TABLE OF CONTENTS

ACRONYMS

AAR	After Action Review
ACLU	American Civil Liberties Union
AEF	Army Expeditionary Forces
APL	American Protective League
ASD(C3I)	Assistant Secretary of Defense for Command, Control, Communications and Intelligence
ATSD(IO)	Assistant to the Secretary of Defense for Intelligence Oversight
CBRNE	Chemical, Biological, Radiological, Nuclear, and High-Yield Explosives
CCMRF	CBRNE Consequence Management Response Force
CIA	Central Intelligence Agency
CIFA	Counterintelligence Field Activity
CJCS	Chairman of the Joint Chiefs of Staff
DCHIC	Defense Counterintelligence and Human Intelligence Center
DHS	Department of Homeland Security
DIA	Defense Intelligence Agency
DNI	Director of National Intelligence
DoD	Department of Defense
DoD IG	Department of Defense Inspector General
DoJ	Department of Justice
FBI	Federal Bureau of Investigation
FISA	Foreign Intelligence Surveillance Act
GAO	Government Accountability Office
GEN	General

HSIN	Homeland Security Information Network
IC	Intelligence Community
IRTPA	Intelligence Reform and Terrorism Prevention Act
ISE	Information Sharing Environment
JPEN	Joint Protection Enterprise Network
JRIES	Joint Regional Information Exchange System
JTTF	Joint Terrorism Task Force
MID	Military Intelligence Division
NCTC	National Counter Terrorism Center
NGA	National Geospatial Intelligence Agency
NORTHCOM	United States Northern Command
NRO	National Reconnaissance Office
NSA	National Security Agency
PCA	Posse Comitatus Act
SECDEF	Secretary of Defense
USC	United States Code
USG	United States Government

ILLUSTRATIONS

CHAPTER 1

INTRODUCTION

One of the most difficult tasks in a free society like our own is the correlation between adequate intelligence to guarantee our nation's security on the one hand, and the preservation of basic human rights on the other.
— U.S. Attorney General Griffin Bell, 1977

When a government wishes to deprive its citizens of freedom, and reduce them to slavery, it generally makes use of a standing army.
— Max Farrand, *The Records of the Federal Convention of 1787*

Since the founding of the United States, citizens have looked with suspicion on the use of federal military forces in domestic operations. Having just freed themselves of an oppressive British Army, the Founding Fathers made the following mandate in the Bill of Rights: "No Soldier shall, in time of peace be quartered in any house, without the consent of the Owner, nor in time of war, but in a manner to be prescribed by law."[1] This declaration was a reflection of America's belief that military authority should never supplant civil authority.

Since 11 September 2001, however, the Executive Branch and, more specifically, the Department of Defense (DoD), have been under enormous pressure to protect the homeland. In the weeks immediately following the attacks, legislators and their constituents were willing to sacrifice some individual civil liberties in order to prevent another domestic attack. This culminated in the passage of the USA Patriot Act in

---

[1] U.S. Constitution, amend. 3.

October 2001.[2] The Patriot Act included several provisions that gave the President unprecedented authority to collect intelligence information on Americans for the purpose of rooting out terrorists and preventing future attacks. Subsequently, the *National Defense Authorization Act of 2007* included a provision authorizing the President to "restore public order and enforce the laws" in the wake of a natural disaster or terrorist attack.[3] Critics argued the law effectively repealed the long-standing Posse Comitatus Act (PCA), which prohibits the use of federal forces in law enforcement functions during domestic operations. However, in reality, the law was little more than a clarification of the existing exceptions to the PCA.

In the years that followed, many believed that the sweeping powers given to the President were not necessary to secure the homeland. As a result, Congress repealed the previous year's perceived expansion of the PCA, as well as several provisions of the Patriot Act.[4] With the election of President Obama came sweeping reviews of all Bush Administration policies and procedures. Surprisingly, this review led to only modest shifts in policy, indicating that the business of securing the homeland is still a top priority.

Throughout this change, the DoD has surprisingly taken on a more prominent role in defense support of civil authorities (DSCA) operations. The first large development in

---

[2] *USA Patriot Act of 2001*, Public Law 107-56, *U.S. Statutes at Large* 115 (2001): 272.

[3] *John Warner National Defense Authorization Act for Fiscal Year 2007*, Public Law 109-364, *U.S. Statutes at Large* 120 (2006): 2083.

[4] *National Defense Authorization Act for Fiscal Year 2008*, Public Law 110-181, *U.S. Statutes at Large* 122 (2008): 23.

this arena came with the establishment of the United States Northern Command

(NORTHCOM) in 2002. The mission of NORTHCOM is to "provide command and

control of Department of Defense (DOD) homeland defense efforts and to coordinate

defense support of civil authorities."[5] In this capacity, NORTHCOM is often faced with

the challenge of conducting domestic military operations within the confines of the PCA.

In addition to the creation of NORTHCOM, the President established an

Information Sharing Environment designed to provide unity of effort among the myriad

of intelligence agencies within the United States.[6] The purpose of this information

sharing initiative was to eliminate perceived stove-piping among federal agencies, and

improve communication between federal and local authorities. To enable this information

sharing, the President created the Information Sharing Council to oversee the intelligence

restructuring.

Amidst these developments, the DoD continues to struggle to integrate State and

local authorities. As recently as September 2009, a Government Accountability Office

report faulted NORTHCOM for not adequately including states in their training exercises

and lessons learned.[7] The reason for this struggle is DoD's uncertainty in the role they

should play in homeland security and cooperation with state and local governments.

---

[5]United States Northern Command, "About U.S. NORTHCOM," http://www.northcom.mil/About/index.html (accessed 17 April 2010).

[6]Executive Order no. 13,311, *Code of Federal Regulations*, title 3, 245 (2004); Executive Order no. 13,388, *Code of Federal Regulations*, title 3, 198 (2006).

[7]United States Government Accountability Office, *Homeland Defense: U.S. Northern Command has a Strong Exercise Program, But Involvement of Interagency Partners and States Can Be Improved* (Washington, DC: Government Printing Office, 2009).

Adding to the confusion is the appropriate role of Army and Air National Guard forces, which can operate in either a state or federal status.

The thesis of this paper will explore whether the PCA is inhibiting the sharing of DoD intelligence information with state and local law enforcement. In support of this thesis, the following subordinate questions will be explored: Must the DoD be involved in gathering intelligence information within the United States? What are the relevant laws and regulations that regulate the gathering and sharing of DoD intelligence? How do these laws restrict sharing of intelligence information? Are these restrictions necessary? Are there other government agencies better suited for this type of intelligence gathering? How does this thesis inform the greater issue of civil-military relations and the origins of Intelligence Oversight?

This research is significant to not only NORTHCOM, but to all of DoD, as well as the Department of Homeland Security (DHS). Cooperation between federal and state authorities is crucial to prevent future terrorist attacks. However, without knowledge of the legal boundaries related to the sharing of information, the DoD will reflexively err on the side of not sharing information. Such a decision could have catastrophic consequences on America's fight against terrorism. In addition, if the thesis identifies gaps in existing law related to DoD intelligence gathering, this research could be used to draft additional legislation to fix those gaps.

The primary underlying assumption in this paper is that America is still susceptible to terrorist attack. Although it has been over eight years since the events of 11 September 2001, the government continues to work with state law enforcement to thwart potential terrorist plots. Additionally, one obvious, although fundamental, assumption is that federal, state, and local law enforcement are all necessary to prevent future domestic attacks. While many believe state and local authorities should continue to play the central role in protecting their jurisdictions, the federal government must continue to support this effort.

My research will be limited to a study of American military forces, and will not include a comparative law component. In addition, I will primarily focus on the collection of intelligence within the United States, and not overseas intelligence collection.

As part of this thesis, I will use several terms specific to homeland security and the DoD. These terms include:

Civil Support. Support to U.S. civil authorities related to domestic emergencies and certain other activities.[8]

Counterintelligence. "Information gathered and activities conducted to protect against espionage, other intelligence activities, sabotage, or assassinations conducted for or on behalf of foreign powers, organizations or persons, or international terrorist activities, but not including personnel, physical, document or communications security programs."[9]

---

[8]Joint Chiefs of Staff, Joint Publication (JP) 3-28, *Civil Support* (Washington, DC: Government Printing Office, 14 September 2007), GL-6.

[9]Department of the Army, Field Manual (FM) 2-22.2, *Counterintelligence* (Washington, DC: Government Printing Office, 21 October 2009), 3-1.

Defense Support of Civil Authorities. Civil support provided in accordance with the National Response Plan.[10]

Domestic emergencies. "Emergencies affecting the public welfare and occurring within the 50 states, District of Columbia, Commonwealth of Puerto Rico, US possessions and territories, or any political subdivision thereof, as a result of enemy attack, insurrection, civil disturbance, earthquake, fire, flood, or other public disasters or equivalent emergencies that endanger life and property or disrupt the usual process of government. Domestic emergencies include civil defense emergencies, civil disturbances, major disasters, and natural disasters."[11]

Domestic intelligence. Information gathered, analyzed, and distributed within the United States and its territories.

Fusion Center. A cell containing representatives of federal, state, and/or local agencies designed to analyze, prevent and investigate criminal or terrorist activity.[12]

Homeland Defense. "the protection of United States sovereignty, territory, domestic population, and critical defense infrastructure against external threats and aggression or other threats as directed by the President."[13]

---

[10]Department of Defense, *DoD Dictionary of Military Terms*, http://www.dtic.mil/doctrine/dod_dictionary/ (accessed 22 April 2010).

[11]Joint Chiefs of Staff, Joint Publication (JP) 3-27, *Homeland Defense* (Washington, DC: Government Printing Office, 12 July 2007), GL-8.

[12]Todd Masse, Siobhan O'Neill, and John Rollins, CRS Report, *Fusion Centers: Issues and Options for Congress* (Washington, DC: Government Printing Office, 2008), 1.

[13]Department of Defense, *DoD Dictionary of Military Terms*.

Homeland Security. "A concerted national effort to prevent terrorist attacks within the United States; reduce America's vulnerability to terrorism, major disasters, and other emergencies; and minimize the damage and recover from attacks, major disasters, and other emergencies that occur."[14]

Homeland Security Intelligence. Integration of foreign and domestic intelligence to obtain seamless intelligence.

Information Sharing Environment. "An approach that facilitates the sharing of terrorism and homeland security information which may include any method determined necessary and appropriate for carrying out" the law.[15]

Intelligence Oversight. "The process of ensuring that all DoD intelligence, counterintelligence, and intelligence related activities are conducted in accordance with applicable U.S. law, Presidential Executive Orders, and DoD directives and regulations."[16]

NORTHCOM. United States Northern Command; a combatant command established to "provide command and control of Department of Defense (DoD) homeland defense efforts and to coordinate defense support of civil authorities."[17]

---

[14]Ibid.

[15]*U.S. Code* 6 (2008), § 485.

[16]Assistant to the Secretary of Defense for Intelligence Oversight, "Frequently Asked Questions," http://atsdio.defense.gov/faq.html (accessed 22 April 2010).

[17]United States Northern Command, "About U.S. NORTHCOM."

CHAPTER 2

LITERATURE REVIEW

This literature review consists of three sections, each addressing a major component of the DoD domestic intelligence issue. The first section discusses the domestic intelligence structure and how DoD relates to that overall structure. The second section explores the Posse Comitatus Act (PCA) and related laws that restrict DoD domestic operations and intelligence gathering. Finally, section three discusses additional laws related to intelligence gathering in the United States.

Overview

The majority of the research in this area will be either legal or military specific. The thesis will provide background by reviewing the U.S. Domestic Intelligence structure as it exists today. Then, the thesis will explore the Posse Comitatus Act (PCA) and the myriad of laws and interpretations that extend from this law. In addition, a large survey of existing DoD Directives and contemporaneous position papers will provide context regarding the DoD's struggle to define the problem of sharing intelligence information gathered in a domestic setting. Finally, the thesis will describe the ancillary laws that regulate intelligence gathering.

The thesis will rely on a significant amount of research from outside of the Department of Defense in order to present alternative opinions. Federal court interpretations, the Congressional Research Service, and numerous law review articles will provide diverging views from those advanced by the DoD.

In addition to legal research, the thesis will rely on military documents to define and explain DoD's role in homeland security. In addition, with the creation of NORTHCOM, many articles have been written about the actual and perceived role of federal military assets in protecting the homeland. Finally, the Government Accountability Office (GAO) and RAND Corporation have completed several studies on homeland security that will be beneficial to developing the thesis.

One major limitation to the research for this topic is that homeland security, as we currently know it, is a relatively dynamic area, with significant changes emerging on a frequent basis. The vast majority of resources will be relatively recent and subject to frequent and perhaps significant change.

Evolution of the U.S. Domestic Intelligence Structure

Domestic intelligence in the United States has a storied past. Although agents of the United States have collected intelligence since the creation of the country, the birth of the modern intelligence structure can be traced to the *National Security Act of 1947*.[18] Prior to the *National Security Act*, intelligence was conducted primarily by the Army and the State Department.[19] This sweeping legislation "provided for a Secretary of Defense, a National Military Establishment, Central Intelligence Agency, and National Security

---

[18]*National Security Act of 1947*, Public Law 80-235, *U.S. Statutes at Large* 61 (1947): 496, codified at *U.S. Code* 50 (2008) § 401 et seq.

[19]Rand Corporation, *The Challenge of Domestic Intelligence in a Free Society*, ed. Brian A. Jackson (Santa Monica: Rand Corporation, 2009), 31.

Resources Board."[20] Despite this comprehensive overhaul of the intelligence structure, the legislation failed to provide for meaningful coordination between the different intelligence agencies.[21]

Over the course of the past sixty years, Congress and the Executive have struggled to remedy this omission in the legislation by establishing a coherent intelligence structure. In 1981, President Reagan issued *Executive Order 12333*, which among other changes, established the U.S. Intelligence Community (IC).[22] Comprised of seventeen Executive Agencies, the IC works "both independently and collaboratively to gather the intelligence necessary to conduct foreign relations and national security activities."[23] The IC was an early step toward the intelligence information-sharing many believed was needed to protect the homeland.

---

[20]Office of the Historian, Bureau of Public Affairs, United States Department of State, "History of the National Security Council: 1947-1997," U.S. Department of State, http://ftp.fas.org/irp.offdocs/ NSChistory.htm (accessed 10 January 2010).

[21]James R. Locher III, "The Most Important Thing: Legislative Reform of the National Security System," *Military Review* 88, no. 3 (May-June 2008): 20.

[22]Executive Order no. 12,333, *Code of Federal Regulations*, title 3, 200 (1982) (Amended by Executive Order no. 13,284, *Code of Federal Regulations*, title 3, 161 (2004); Executive Order no. 13,355, *Code of Federal Regulations*, title 3, 218 (2005); and Executive Order 13,470, *Federal Register* 73, no. 150 (4 August 2008): 45325.

[23]Director of National Intelligence, "About the Intelligence Community: Seventeen Agencies and Organizations United Under One Goal," Office of the Director of National Intelligence, http://www.intelligence.gov/about-the-intelligence-community/ (accessed 20 January 2010). The seventeen member agencies are: Air Force Intelligence; Army Intelligence; Central Intelligence Agency; Coast Guard Intelligence; Defense Intelligence Agency; Department of Energy; Department of Homeland Security; Department of State; Department of the Treasury; Drug Enforcement Administration; Federal Bureau of Investigation; Marine Corps Intelligence; National Geospatial-Intelligence Agency; National Reconnaissance Office; National Security Agency; Navy Intelligence; Office of the Director of National Intelligence. Ibid.

Just seven months prior to the 11 September attacks, the U.S. Commission on National Security published the results of a two-year study of the Nation's national security challenges. In *Road Map for National Security: Imperative for Change*, the Commission made an ominous prediction: "The combination of unconventional weapons proliferation with the persistence of international terrorism will end the relative invulnerability of the U.S. homeland to catastrophic attack. A direct attack against American citizens on American soil is likely over the next quarter century."[24] The Commission recommended a comprehensive overhaul of America's homeland security structure, including adopting a "strategy of layered defense that focuses first on prevention, second on protection, and third on response."[25] An integral part of this strategy was the need for information sharing between intelligence agencies.

The attacks of 11 September brought new urgency to the effort to reorganize the intelligence community. The President quickly undertook a rapid overhaul of the intelligence structure.[26] However, the most comprehensive changes came in response to the 9/11 Commission's recommendations. In the 9/11 Report, the Commission attributed the intelligence community's failure to detect and prevent the attacks of 11 September to

---

[24]The United States Commission on National Security/21st Century, *Road Map for National Security: Imperative for Change* (Washington, DC: Government Printing Office, 2001), x.

[25]Ibid.

[26]The establishment of the Department of Homeland Security and the Homeland Security Council was just one of the actions that greatly affected intelligence sharing among federal agencies. Executive Order 13,228, *Code of Federal Regulations*, title 3, 796 (2002).

11

a lack of information sharing.[27] As a result, Congress passed the *Intelligence Reform and Terrorism Prevention Act (IRTPA)*, which among other changes, established the position of Director of National Intelligence (DNI). [28] The DNI's main duties are to coordinate the efforts of U.S. intelligence agencies. Specifically, the "DNI establishes objectives and priorities for the intelligence community and manages and directs tasking of collection, analysis, production, and dissemination of national intelligence."[29] Prior to the creation of the DNI, the Director of Central Intelligence oversaw both the Intelligence Community and the Central Intelligence Agency.[30] For the first time in history, the U.S. intelligence community is now led by a separate director with the ability to transcend agency cultures and coordinate comprehensive intelligence support.

---

[27]United States Senate Committee on Governmental Affairs, *Summary of Intelligence Reform and Terrorism Prevention Act of 2004* (Washington, DC: Government Printing Office, 2004), 5-6; U.S. National Commission on Terrorist Attacks Upon the United States, *The 9/11 Commission Report: Final Report* (Washington, DC: Government Printing Office, 2004).

[28]*Intelligence Reform and Terrorism Prevention Act (IRTPA)*, Public Law 108-458, *U.S. Statutes at Large* 118 (2004): 3638. In 2007, Congress amended the *IRTPA* to specifically include homeland security and weapons of mass destruction within the ISE's scope. *Implementing Recommendations of the 9/11 Commission Act of 2007*, Public Law 110-53, *U.S. Statutes at Large* 121 (2007): 266; U.S. Department of Justice, "Privacy & Civil Liberties: Federal Statutes Relevant in the Information Sharing Environment," U.S. Department of Justice, http://www. It.ojp.gov/ default.aspx?area=privacy&page=1283 (accessed 20 January 2010).

[29]United States Senate Committee on Governmental Affairs, 2-3.

[30]Ibid., 1; Director of National Intelligence, "About the Intelligence Community: A Complex Organization United Under a Single Goal: National Security," Office of the Director of National Intelligence, http://www.intelligence.gov/about-the-intelligence-community/structure/ (accessed 19 April 2010).

In addition to establishing the DNI, Congress also reinforced the President's earlier initiatives to improve sharing of terrorism information.[31] Congress directed the President to establish an Information Sharing Environment (ISE), with the mission of "facilitat[ing] the sharing of terrorism information among all appropriate Federal, State, local, tribal and private sector entities, through the use of policy guidelines and technologies."[32] The resulting ISE Program Manager and Information Sharing Council are tasked with providing recommendations to the President on information sharing policy and ensure proper coordination among the various members of the ISE.[33]

Finally, the *IRTPA* codified the President's creation of the National Counterterrorism Center.[34] The purpose of the NCTC is to serve "as the primary organization in the United States Government (USG) for integrating and analyzing *all* intelligence pertaining to counterterrorism (except for information pertaining exclusively to domestic terrorism)."[35] The NCTC is staffed by members of the various intelligence agencies, and performs both joint planning and joint intelligence analysis.[36] The

---

[31]Executive Order 13,356, *Code of Federal Regulations*, title 3, 223 (2005). This Executive Order was later revoked by Executive Order 13,388, *Code of Federal Regulations*, title 3, 198 (2006).

[32]United States Senate Committee on Governmental Affairs, 5-6.

[33]Executive Order no. 13,388, 198.

[34]*Intelligence Reform and Terrorism Prevention Act*, 214.

[35]National Counterterrorism Center, "About the National Counterterrorism Center," National Counterterrorism Center, http://www.nctc.gov/about_us/about_nctc.html (accessed 19 April 2010).

[36]Ibid.

intelligence products created by the NCTC are distributed throughout the intelligence community and government. The NCTC, along with the Information Sharing Environment and Director of National Intelligence, represent an extraordinary effort on behalf of the government to facilitate information sharing between all levels of government.

Current Intelligence Structure

The U.S. Government's substantial restructuring of the intelligence infrastructure has yielded a more complex, but less stove-piped organization. The various intelligence agencies of the Intelligence Community can be divided into three groupings: the program managers, departmental, and services groups (see figure 1). The first group, the "program managers," consist of the independent intelligence departments. The "departmental," however, consist of "IC components within government departments outside the Department of Defense that focus on serving their parent department's intelligence needs."[37] Finally, the "Services" level consists of intelligence agencies that serve their parent military branch. Together, these intelligence agencies provide intelligence support to government leaders and the military.

---

[37]Director of National Intelligence, "About the Intelligence Community: A Complex Organization United Under a Single Goal: National Security," Office of the Director of National Intelligence, http://www.intelligence.gov/about-the-intelligence-community/structure/ (accessed 19 April 2010).

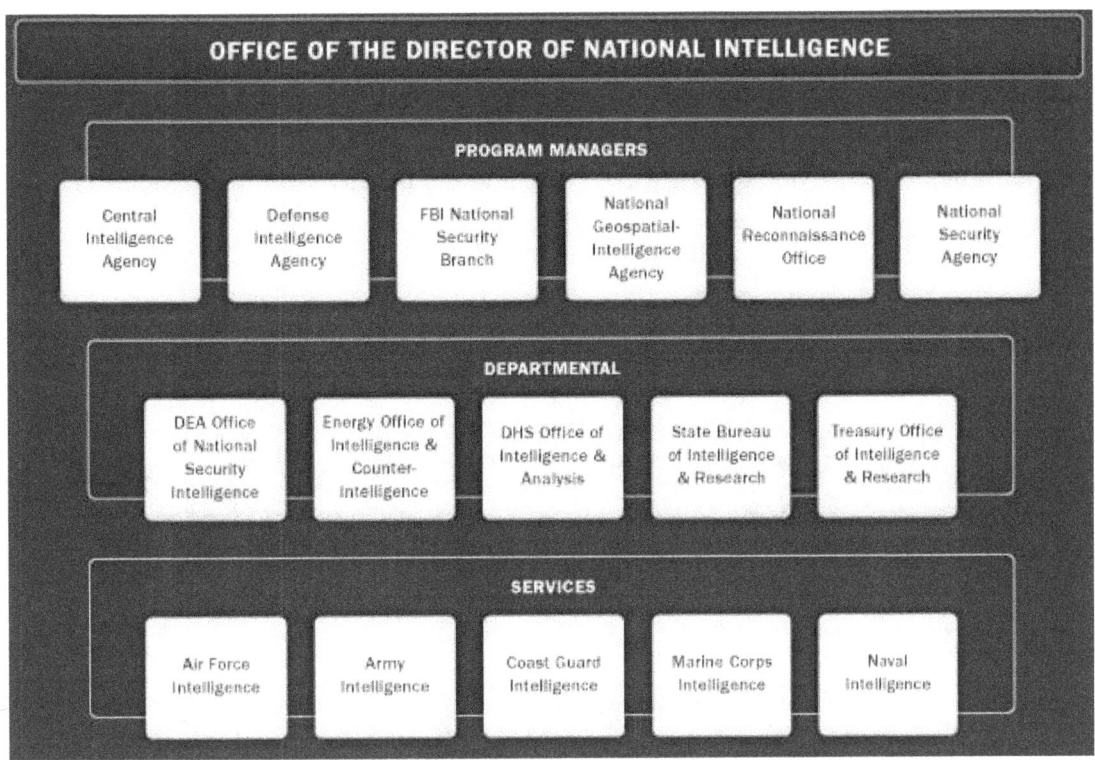

Figure 1. Structure of the Intelligence Community.
Source: Intelligence Community, "About the Intelligence Community: Seventeen Agencies and Organizations United Under One Goal," http://www.intelligence.gov/about-the-intelligence-community/ (accessed 20 January 2010).

Although several federal agencies possess intelligence capabilities, the vast majority of intelligence assets fall under the control of the Secretary of Defense (SECDEF) (See figure 2). In fact, the DoD accounts for the vast majority of the $49.8 billion yearly intelligence budget.[38] In managing this large apparatus, the SECDEF is supported by the Assistant Secretary of Defense for Command, Control, Communications

[38]Richard A. Best, Jr., CRS Report for Congress, *Intelligence Community Reorganization: Potential Effects on DoD Intelligence Agencies* (Washington, DC: Government Printing Office, 2004), 1; Director of National Intelligence, "News Release: DNI Releases Budget Figure for 2009 National Intelligence Program," 30 October 2009, http://www.dni.gov/press_releases/20091030_release.pdf (accessed 20 April 2010).

and Intelligence (ASD(C3I)). In addition, the SECDEF receives substantive intelligence support from the Defense Intelligence Agency (DIA).[39] The DIA identifies and coordinates department-wide intelligence needs, and the Director of the DIA reports to both the SECDEF and the Chairman of the Joint Chiefs of Staff (CJCS) in his role as the CJCS's intelligence advisor.[40]

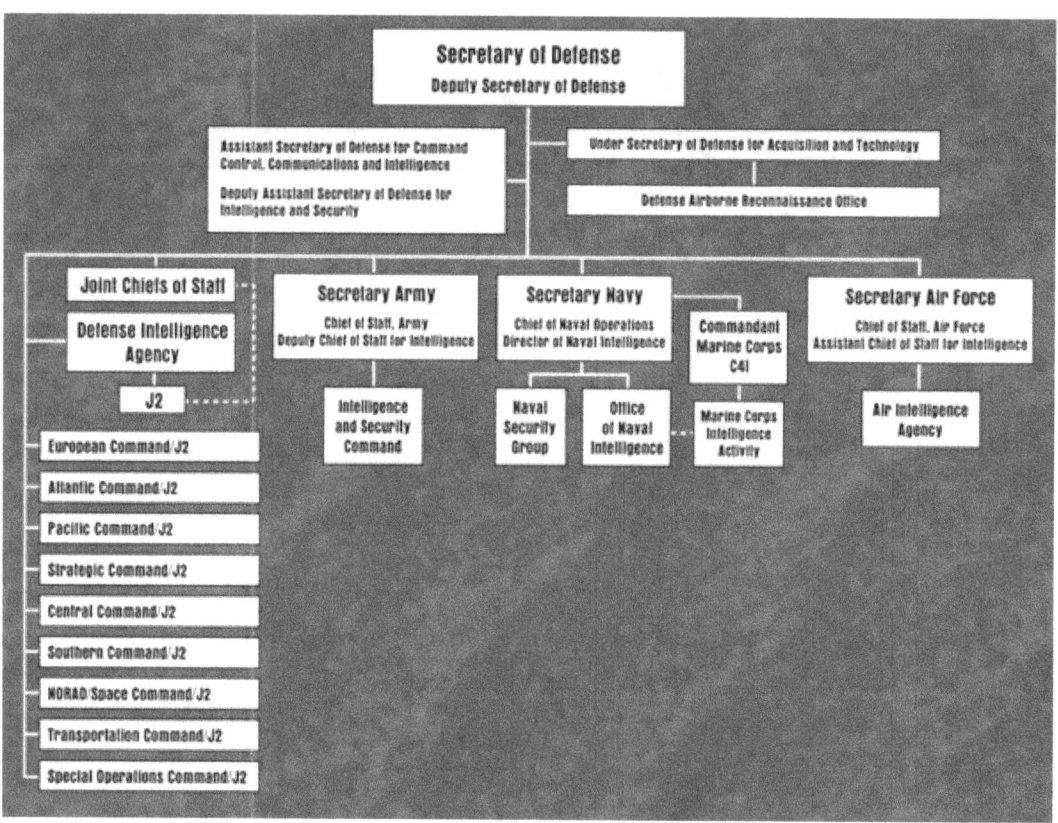

Figure 2.   Military Intelligence Structure

Source: www.gpo.gov

---

[39]Federation of American Scientists, "Intelligence Resource Program: Military Intelligence," http://www.fas.org/ irp/offdocs/int014.html (accessed 20 January 2010).

[40]Ibid.

Beyond the DIA, the Unified Commands are "charged with developing plans, programs, and architectures to ensure that intelligence capabilities are available, interoperable, and can be employed in support of joint operations."[41] In addition, the military departments provide both strategic and tactical intelligence.[42] With these considerable assets, the DoD plays a crucial role in gathering and analyzing both foreign and domestic intelligence.

Information Sharing

As discussed previously, the centerpiece of intelligence restructuring is information sharing. In 2007, the Bush Administration published the first *National Strategy for Information Sharing*, reinforcing the notion that "[t]he exchange of information should be the rule, not the exception, in our efforts to combat the terrorist threat."[43] The document reinforces the importance of leveraging information provided by all levels of government, the private sector, and foreign partners to combat terrorism. It also makes clear that the foundation for this information sharing must be the preservation of individual rights.[44]

---

[41]Ibid.; Joint Chiefs of Staff, Joint Publication (JP) 2-0, *Joint Intelligence* (Washington, DC: Government Printing Office, 22 June 2007), I-2.

[42]Federation of American Scientists, "Intelligence Resource Program: Military Intelligence."

[43]The White House, *National Strategy for Information Sharing: Successes and Challenges in Improving Terrorism-Related Information Sharing* (Washington, DC: Government Printing Office, 2007), 1.

[44]Ibid., 8.

In 2008, the DNI published the first *Information Sharing Strategy*.[45] Nested with the President's *National Strategy*, the strategy provides a comprehensive implementation plan to achieve the vision of "[a]n integrated intelligence enterprise that anticipates mission needs for information by making the complete spectrum of intelligence information seamlessly available to support all stages of the intelligence process."[46] As illustrated in Figure 3, the document reinforces a new paradigm for the intelligence community. Namely, agencies will no longer focus exclusively on agency information needs, but rather take on a "responsibility to provide" information to other government agencies. In addition, the strategy calls for uniform information sharing policies among the various agencies to prevent multiple classification systems that inhibit information sharing. Finally, the strategy prefaces all of these initiatives by emphasizing the importance of respecting civil liberties and working within the confines of laws that limit information sharing.[47] The sweeping changes in the *Information Sharing Strategy* are a reflection of the new culture of the intelligence community under the DNI.

---

[45]Director of National Intelligence, *United States Intelligence Community: Information Sharing Strategy* (Washington, DC: Government Printing Office, 2008).

[46]Ibid., 9.

[47]Ibid.

Legacy Information Sharing Model	New Information Sharing Model

① Info Sharing Vision — **"Need to Know"** – The legacy model of sharing intelligence data to trusted parties when deemed necessary by the data provider → **"Responsibility to Provide"** – A new mindset to share intelligence data while still addressing the need to protect privacy, civil liberties, and sources and methods

② Enterprise Scope — **Agency-Centric** – Developed to support a particular agency's needs for particular mission sets → **Enterprise-Centric** – Collaboration/Services marketplace stretches across agencies, partners, and international borders for multiple mission use

③ Collaboration Type — **Static** – Developed in accordance with policies and regulations of particular intelligence product with little change or flexibility → **Mission-Centric "Self Generating"** – Rapidly adapts to changing needs and introduction of new partners (state, local, tribal governments)

④ Security Model — **Network-Centric** – Security designed around each network (e.g., DMZ, firewalls) → **Information-Centric** – Security built into the data and environment, i.e., "security in-depth" (e.g., data tags/XML)

⑤ Access Model — **Compartment-Based** – Access based primarily on security access controls and regulations → **Attribute-Based** – Access based on attributes beyond security classification (e.g., environmental, mission focus, affiliation, etc.)

⑥ Data Usage — **Data "Owner"** – Cultural mindset of intelligence data owned by the providing agency with strict controls on access, distribution, and sharing mechanisms → **Data "Stewardship"** – Cultural shift to intelligence data stewardship to facilitate multi-dimensional analysis and usage with appropriate security protocols

STRATEGIC DRIVERS / DATA & SECURITY DRIVERS

GREATER COLLABORATION

Figure 3.   Military Intelligence Structure
Source: Office of the Director of National Intelligence, *United States Intelligence Community: Information Sharing Strategy* (Washington, DC: Government Printing Office, 2008), 9.

Although these documents provide strategy for information sharing at all levels, both documents dedicate a substantial section to information sharing between federal and state and local law enforcement. A crucial component of this information sharing effort is state and urban area fusion centers.[48] Fusion centers are responsible for coordinating "the gathering, analysis, and dissemination of law enforcement, homeland security, public safety, and terrorism information."[49] They serve as the central clearinghouse for

---

[48]The White House, *National Strategy for Information Sharing*, 20.

[49]Ibid.

information provided by Federal, as well as other state intelligence sources. Over the course of the past several years, states have stood up over 40 fusion centers throughout the country. In an effort to lend some standardization to fusion centers, the Department of Justice issued detailed guidelines for the establishment and operation of fusion centers in 2006.[50] Coupled with the Federal interagency information sharing initiatives, these fusion centers provide a central processing point at the state-level capable of leveraging the full complement of U.S. intelligence assets.

Many critics of information sharing focus on the dangers inherent in fusion centers. The American Civil Liberties Union (ACLU) argues that what started as a means to combat terrorism has turned into an "all crimes and all hazards" information sharing operation.[51] As a result, all agencies now have sufficient information to create a detailed profile of American citizens. Multiple agency involvement, coupled with ambiguous lines of authority and military participation, make fusion centers ripe for abuse. The standards promulgated by the Department of Justice attempt to remedy some of the concerns articulated by the ACLU and others. Despite these criticisms, the information sharing transformation launched by the DNI has attempted to leverage the substantial intelligence assets available at all levels of government to prevent terrorism.

---

[50]Department of Justice, *Fusion Center Guidelines: Developing and Sharing Information and Intelligence in a New Era* (Washington, DC: Government Printing Office, 2006).

[51]American Civil Liberties Union, "What's Wrong with Fusion Centers?," http://aclu.org/pdfs/privacy/fusioncenter_20071212.pdf (accessed 27 April 2010).

Relevant Law Governing Domestic Intelligence

The *Posse Comitatus Act*

As discussed in the introduction, Americans have always been leery of a large standing army and particularly uncomfortable when that army collects domestic intelligence. This suspicion most likely derives from the concept of posse comitatus, a term that has its origins in British Common Law. The specter of martial law was roundly denounced by William Blackstone in his influential Commentaries on the Laws of England. In this 1765 seminal work, Blackstone condemned martial law as "in truth and reality no law, but something indulged, rather than allowed as a law. . . ."[52] In America, the British used the military for law enforcement missions, most notably in the case of the Boston Massacre, when British troops fired on rioting civilians.[53] Just six years after this incident, in articulating the tyranny brought on by the King of England, the Declaration of Independence stated: "He has affected to render the Military independent of and superior to the Civil power."[54] As a result of these and other abuses, the Constitution provides for substantial due process as outlined in the Fourth Amendment.[55] In addition, the suspicion related to standing militaries is evident in the Third Amendment, which

---

[52]William Blackstone, *Commentaries on the Laws of England*, (1765; repr. Book I, Birmingham: Legal Classics Library, 1983], 400; Stephen Young, "The Posse Comitatus Act: A Resource Guide," 17 February 2003, http://www.llrx.com/features/posse.htm (accessed 20 January 2010).

[53]Stephen Young, "The Posse Comitatus Act: A Resource Guide."

[54]The United States Declaration of Independence; Laird v. Tatum, 408 U.S. 19 (1972).

[55]U.S. Constitution, amend. 4.

strictly limits the circumstances under which the military can quarter troops in private houses.[56] Despite these restrictions, however, Article II, Section VIII, does allow the use of the military "to execute the Laws of the Union, suppress Insurrections and repel Invasions. . . ."[57] Over time, these protections have evolved into a deep rooted belief that "[t]he primary responsibility for protecting life and property and maintaining law and order in the civilian community is vested in the State and local governments."[58] Despite these traditions, however, the use of federal forces in domestic operations has steadily expanded over time.

The origin of the concept of posse comitatus in federal law is *The Judiciary Act of 1789*.[59] The act established inferior federal courts in accordance with Article III of the Constitution, as well as U.S. Marshals, empowering them to use a posse comitatus to enforce laws.[60] Three years later, the *Calling Forth Act* specifically authorized the President to use military forces to quell insurrections within the United States.[61] After

---

[56]U.S. Constitution, amend. 3.

[57]U.S. Constitution, art. 2, sec. 8; Stephen Young, "The Posse Comitatus Act: A Resource Guide."

[58]Department of Defense, Directive 3025.12, "Military Assistance for Civil Disturbances (MACDIS)" (Washington, DC: Government Printing Office, 4 February 1994), 3.

[59]Charles Warren, "New Light on the History of the Federal Judiciary Act of 1789," *Harvard Law Review* 37 (November 1923): 49. *The Judiciary Act* was "Senate bill No. 1, in the First Session of the First Congress." Ibid.

[60]Donald J. Currier, *The Posse Comitatus Act: A Harmless Relic from the Post-Reconstruction Era or a Legal Impediment to Transformation?* (Carlisle: Strategic Studies Institute, 2003), 2.

employment during the Whiskey Rebellion and in enforcing the *Fugitive Slave Act*, the use of federal forces to enforce the law steadily became a point of contention among lawmakers.[62]

Following the Civil War, federal troops maintained a heavy presence in Southern states to the consternation of many Southerners. The issue came to a head in the particularly contentious election of 1876. Democrat Samuel Tilden led the popular vote by nearly 250,000 over Republican Rutherford Hayes, but Hayes led the electoral vote by one.[63]. After several months of negotiations, Southern Democrats agreed to not contest the election results in exchange for Hayes withdrawing federal troops from the South.[64] The resulting legislation was the *Posse Comitatus Act of 1878*.[65] The Act provides:

> Whoever, except in cases and under circumstances expressly authorized by the Constitution or Act of Congress, willfully uses any part of the Army or the Air Force as a posse comitatus or otherwise to execute the laws shall be fined under this title or imprisoned not more than two years, or both.[66]

---

[61]Matt Matthews, *The Posse Comitatus Act and the United States Army: A Historical Perspective* (Fort Leavenworth: Combat Studies Institute Press, 2006), 7.

[62]Ibid., 8.

[63]Congressional Quarterly, *Presidential Elections: 1789-2004* (Washington, DC: CQ Press, 2005), 187.

[64]Ibid.; Sydney I. Pomerantz, "Election of 1876," in *History of Presidential Elections*, ed. Arthur M. Schlesinger, Jr. (New York: Chelsea House, 1971), 2: 1379.

[65]Colonel Chris R. Gentry, "Self-Evident Truths: Why We Can Stop Worrying and Love the Posse Comitatus Act" (Research Paper, Army War College, 2008), 6.

[66]*U.S. Code* 18 (2008), § 1385.

This criminal statute has changed little from the time it was drafted in 1878, with the exception of an update to apply the PCA to all branches of Service.[67] However, as will be discussed in chapter 4, the spirit and meaning of the PCA has evolved significantly over the past 130 years.

The Boundaries of the PCA

The Federal courts have wrestled with the meaning and application of the PCA almost from its inception. From First Amendment implications to the authority of military police on military installations, the standards continue to evolve. One of the seminal cases in this area is Laird v. Tatum,[68] in which a group of U.S. citizens brought a class action lawsuit against the Department of Defense alleging First Amendment violations. In the suit, the class argued that the Department of the Army's "'surveillance of lawful and peaceful civilian political activity'" was a violation of the PCA, and resulted in a chilling effect that dissuaded individuals from participating in war protests.[69]

The genesis of this domestic intelligence-gathering program was the widespread civil unrest experienced in many American cities in 1967. In response to the rioting, President Johnson invoked the *Insurrection Act* to send federal troops to quell the

---

[67]*U.S. Statutes at Large* 70a (1956): 626 (amending the PCA to include Air Force); Department of Defense, Directive 5525.5, "DoD Cooperation with Civilian Law Enforcement Officials"(Washington DC: Government Printing Office, 15 January 1986) (incorporating change 1, 20 December 1989).

[68]Laird v. Tatum, 408 U.S. 1 (1972).

[69]Ibid., 2.

violence in Detroit.[70] After the incident, the Army realized that they required an

intelligence database that would provide them situational awareness on U.S. urban

centers in the event they were called to quell another insurrection. As a result, the Army

developed a data-gathering system that would assist in contingency planning for domestic

response.[71]

Although the central holding in Laird was that the class did not present a

justiciable controversy,[72] in so holding, the Court endorsed the Army's data-collection

program, arguing that such information was necessary to providing timely and

responsible support in the event of a domestic insurrection.[73] The dissent vehemently

disagreed with the holding of the Court, however, arguing that:

> If Congress had passed a law authorizing the armed services to establish
> surveillance over the civilian population, a most serious constitutional problem
> would be presented. There is, however, no law authorizing surveillance over
> civilians, which in this case the Pentagon concededly had undertaken. The
> question is whether such authority may be implied. One can search the
> Constitution in vain for any such authority.[74]

In apparent reaction to Laird and other cases, AR 381-10, *U.S. Army Intelligence*

Activities, now specifically caveats the chapter dealing with collecting information on

---

[70]Ibid., 4-5.

[71]Ibid., 5.

[72]The Court specifically held that: the jurisdiction of a federal court may [not] be
invoked by a complainant who alleges that the exercise of his First Amendment rights is
being chilled by the mere existence, without more, of a governmental investigative and
data-gathering activity that is alleged to be broader in scope than is reasonably necessary
for the accomplishment of a valid governmental purpose. Ibid., 10.

[73]Ibid., 5-6.

[74]Ibid., 16 (Douglas, J. Dissenting).

U.S. Persons with the following disclaimer: "First Amendment protection: Nothing is this procedure will be interpreted as authorizing the collection of any information relating to a U.S. person solely because of that person's lawful advocacy of measures opposed to Government policy." Despite such clarification, disagreements over the role of the Department of Defense in domestic intelligence would continue in later cases.

The courts have clearly established certain aspects of the PCA, particularly the military's power to conduct law enforcement on federal installations. In United States v. Banks, military police searched and arrested a civilian for heroin possession on a military reservation.[75] On appeal, the defendant argued that the military lacked the power to arrest civilians for civil offenses. He argued that the military's actions in enforcing civil law was a violation of the PCA. The Ninth Circuit clearly rejected this argument, stating that "the power to maintain order, security and discipline on a military reservation is necessary to military operations."[76] Although the courts have clearly established the military's authority to enforce laws on military reservations, the boundaries of military law enforcement in the civilian community are less certain.

The Wounded Knee Cases

In February 1973, members of the "American Indian Movement" raided a town on a South Dakota Indian Reservation called Wounded Knee, looting the stores and

---

[75]United States v. Banks, 539 F.2d 14, 15 (9th Cir. 1976).

[76]Ibid., 16.

taking hostages.[77] After a protracted standoff, active duty Army officers were called in to provide assistance to the Federal Bureau of Investigations (FBI), the United States Marshals, and the Bureau of Indian Affairs, who were dealing with the crisis.[78] The extent of military involvement included: use of Army materiel and equipment; presence of Army personnel to observe, report, and consult on resolving the crisis; advice on the rules of engagement and planning of operations; and aerial photographic reconnaissance of the area.[79] As a result of the incident, several individuals were arrested and prosecuted for interfering with federal law enforcement's efforts to restore order.[80]

In the resulting cases, the federal district courts wrestled with the issue of whether the Army's involvement at Wounded Knee constituted "execut[ing] the laws" as stated in the PCA. Consequently, at least two courts devised tests for whether military involvement violates the PCA. In United States v. Red Feather, the court held that "to execute the laws" means "use of federal military troops in an active role of direct law enforcement by civil law enforcement officers."[81] The court went on to define active role as "arrest; seizure of evidence; search of a person; search of a building; investigation of crime; interviewing witnesses; pursuit of an escaped civilian prisoner; search of an area

---

[77]See for example, United States v. Jaramillo, 380 F.Supp 1375, 1377 (D. Neb. 1974).

[78]Ibid., 1377.

[79]United States v. Red Feather, 392 F.Supp. 921 (D. S.D. 1975).

[80]See for example, Ibid.

[81]Ibid., 925.

for a suspect and other like activities."[82] This detailed definition, however, would be squarely rejected by another court.

In United States v. Jamarillo, a different court faced with the same facts reinforced the notion that mere presence of Army personnel does not rise to the level of a PCA violation.[83] The court held that "actual use [of] the Army or the Air Force to execute the laws" is the true prohibited conduct.[84] However, the court goes on to state that if Army personnel influenced the Department of Justice (DOJ) and the other agencies present in their decision-making, then a violation of the PCA may have occurred.[85] In other words, the court held that if the Army provides advice to the federal agents, and the agents accept and implement that advice, then the Army would be "executing the laws" and violating the PCA. This rather liberal definition of the term "use of the Army" resulted in the court acquitting the defendants in the Jamarillo case because the PCA violation meant that the law enforcement was not "lawfully engaged in the lawful performance of official duties."[86] While both the Jamarillo and Red Feather cases provide some clarification on the definition of the PCA, the various courts' interpretations of these definitions are vastly different.

---

[82]Ibid.

[83]United States v. Jaramillo, 380 F.Supp 1375, 1380 (D. Neb. 1974).

[84]Ibid.

[85]Ibid.

[86]Ibid., 1378.

Exceptions to the PCA

The PCA is generally interpreted to prohibit the use of federal troops in a direct, domestic law enforcement capacity.[87] Congress has, however, passed several exceptions to the PCA. Specifically, 10 USC 331, et seq., also known as the *Insurrection Act*, allows the use of federal troops in order to restore order in the event of an insurrection.[88] Although the *Insurrection Act* grants sweeping authority to the President to deploy federal troops in response to an insurrection, the Act has rarely been invoked. President George H.W. Bush was the last Commander-in-Chief to invoke the *Insurrection Act*, when he deployed federal troops in response to the Los Angeles Riots.[89] However, even in that case, the federal troops were not used in a law enforcement capacity because of confusion over the meaning of the PCA.[90]

In addition to the *Insurrection Act*, 10 USC 371, et seq. allows federal military forces to provide support to federal, state, and local law enforcement agencies.[91] Among the support authorized under the statute, 10 USC 371 specifically authorizes the DoD to provide "information" to federal, state, and local law enforcement "collected during the normal course of military training or operations that may be relevant to a violation of any

---

[87]Gentry, 2.

[88]*U.S. Code* 10 (2010), § 331.

[89]See for example, James Delk, *Fires and Furies: The L.A. Riots: What Really Happened* (Palm Springs: ETC Publications, 1995).

[90]Ibid., 111.

[91]*U.S. Code* 10 (2010), § 371, et seq.

Federal or State law within the jurisdiction of such officials."[92] However, the DoD is restricted to providing this information only "in accordance with other applicable law."[93] Therefore, the PCA appears to restrict the sharing of intelligence information in many situations.

Finally, the DoD recognizes an additional limited exception to the PCA. Termed "emergency authority," the provision allows for

> [P]rompt and vigorous Federal action, including use of military forces, to prevent loss of life or wanton destruction of property and to restore governmental functioning and public order when sudden and unexpected civil disturbances, disaster, or calamities seriously endanger life and property and disrupt normal governmental functions to such an extent that duly constituted local authorities are unable to control the situation.[94]

This emergency authority authorizes use of force when necessary, and therefore is exercised only under the most extreme conditions, when there is no time to gain the permission of higher headquarters, and only at the request of local authorities.[95] In addition, the assistance must be of limited duration and the request must be reported

---

[92] *U.S. Code* 10 (2010), § 371. Department of Defense, DoDD 5525.5 goes one step farther, stating that Military Departments and Defense Agencies are not only authorized, but "encouraged" to provide such information to civilian law enforcement agencies.

[93] Department of Defense, Directive 5525.5.

[94] Department of Defense, Directive 5525.5.; Jennifer K. Elsea and R. Chuck Mason, CRS Report for Congress, *The Use of Federal Troops for Disaster Assistance: Legal Issues* (Washington, DC: Government Printing Office, 2008), 3.

[95] Joint Chiefs of Staff, JP 3-28, *Civil Support*, II-7.

through the chain of command to the National Military Command Center at the earliest possible opportunity.[96]

The Stafford Act

Although not a direct exception to the PCA, the Stafford Act allows the President to use federal forces in response to natural disasters.[97] In order to provide this assistance, the Governor of the affected state must implement the State's emergency plan, determine that the disaster exceeds the capabilities of the State and local government, and make a request to the President.[98] The Stafford Act authorizes the President to provide a host of federal resources to states affected by natural or manmade disasters.[99] Among these resources, the President is authorized to send federal forces to the affected area to conduct disaster relief. The Stafford Act stops short, however, of authorizing the President to employ federal forces in a law enforcement capacity. Although the forces may conduct rescue, recovery, and debris removal, they may not conduct patrols, direct traffic, or perform other law enforcement functions.[100]

---

[96]Ibid.

[97]*Robert T. Stafford Disaster Relief and Emergency Assistance Act*, Public Law 93-288, codified at *U.S. Code* 42 (2008), §§ 5121–5206. For additional discussion of the Stafford Act, see Daniel J. Sennott, "Interpreting Recent Changes to the Standing Rules for the Use of Force," *The Army Lawyer* (November 2007): 65.

[98]*Robert T. Stafford Disaster Relief and Emergency Assistance Act*, § 5170 (major disaster declarations) and § 5191 (emergency declarations).

[99]Elsea and Mason, 4.

[100]Ibid.

In addition to the powers articulated under the Stafford Act, the DoD advances the concept of "immediate response" to authorize immediate intervention during a disaster.[101] This concept allows military commanders the discretion to respond to requests for assistance from civil authorities absent a Presidential declaration or authorization from higher headquarters.[102] However, such intervention is only authorized under "imminently serious conditions resulting from any civil emergency or attack . . . to save lives, prevent human suffering, or mitigate great property damage."[103] Like the Stafford Act, federal forces are limited to providing rescue, recovery and debris removal assistance, and may not normally conduct law enforcement activities.[104] The Stafford Act and its supporting policies allow the President to provide extensive assistance, but does not provide an exception to the PCA.

Other Laws Governing Domestic Intelligence

The Church Report and Resulting Legislation

In reaction to perceived overreaching by domestic Defense intelligence agencies during the Vietnam War and in the wake of the Watergate scandal, Congress conducted several hearings to investigate intelligence abuses. The most prominent of these hearings was chaired by Senator Frank Church, with such notable vice-chairmen as Senators John

---

[101]Department of Defense, Directive 3025.1, "Military Support to Civil Authorities (MSCA)" (Washington, DC: Government Printing Office, 15 January 1997), 7; Elsea and Mason, 5.

[102]Department of Defense, Directive 3025.1, 7.

[103]Ibid.

[104]Ibid.

Tower, Walter Mondale, and Barry Goldwater.[105] Known as the "Report of the Select

Committee to Study Governmental Operations with respect to Intelligence Activities," or

more simply "The Church Report," the revelations of the hearings were wide in scope

and extremely controversial.[106] The Committee reviewed all of the intelligence agencies

within the United States, the relationships between the various intelligence agencies, and

the relationship between the agencies and foreign powers.

The DoD intelligence apparatus was of particular concern to the Committee. In

fact, much of the motivation for holding the hearings was to investigate DoD's alleged

abuses of power. The Committee noted that the DoD was responsible for 90 percent of

the Nation's intelligence budget, and "[t]he sheer size and complexity of the Defense

intelligence establishment make it difficult to comprehend the problems and issues which

confront policymakers and intelligence managers."[107] Despite this vast network, the

Committee focused on five fundamental issues concerning DoD: resource management of

DoD intelligence; the role of the Defense Intelligence Agency (DIA) in relation to the

CIA; National Security Agency (NSA) monitoring activities; DoD counterintelligence

and investigative activities; and intelligence-related chemical and biological research.[108]

---

[105]Bill Moyers Journal, "The Church Committee and FISA," Public Broadcasting System, 26 October 2007, http://www.pbs.org/moyers/journal/10262007/profile2.html (accessed 12 April 2010).

[106]Senate Select Committee, *Final Report of the Select Committee to Study Governmental Operations with respect to Intelligence Activities (The Church Report)*, 94th Cong., 2d sess., 1976, S. Rep. 94-755.

[107]Ibid., 319.

[108]Ibid.

The Committee found "abuses of authority in all these subject areas."[109] The Committee found that, in several instances, the military violated the PCA by gathering intelligence for law enforcement purposes. This damning pronouncement set the stage for sweeping findings.

The Church Report's most significant findings related to oversight. The Report faulted Congress for failing to establish statutory boundaries that clearly articulate how intelligence agencies can accomplish their mission without violating the PCA and the Constitution.[110] In addition, the Committee recommended

> that new statutory charters for [intelligence] agencies must be written that take account of the experience of the past three and a half decades. Further, the Committee finds that the relationship among the various intelligence agencies and between them and the Director of Central Intelligence should be restructured in order to achieve better accountability, coordination, and more efficient use of resources.[111]

These findings were the basis for two of the most enduring intelligence changes to emerge as a result of the hearings: The *Foreign Intelligence Surveillance Act* (*FISA*) of 1978, and the intelligence oversight apparatus.[112]

The *Foreign Intelligence Surveillance Act* (*FISA*)

Although the *FISA* has received significant media coverage since the 11 September attacks, the genesis of the law dates back to the Watergate Scandal.[113] As

---

[109]Ibid.

[110]Ibid., 425.

[111]Ibid.

[112]Bill Moyers Journal, "The Church Committee and FISA."

President Carter stated at the signing ceremony, the law requires "a prior judicial warrant for *all* electronic surveillance for foreign intelligence or counterintelligence purposes in the United States in which communications of U.S. persons may be intercepted."[114] In his statement, however, President Carter neglected to mention a large exception to the judicial warrant requirement. Under Section 105(e), the Attorney General may authorize the emergency employment of electronic surveillance if: (1) he determines that an emergency situation prevents him from obtaining a prior judicial warrant for electronic surveillance, and (2) the factual basis required to issue a warrant exists.[115] However, even in emergency cases, the Attorney General must notify a judge on the FISA court that the decision has been made, and must follow-up with an application for the warrant.[116]

Despite the *FISA*'s clear regulation of domestic intelligence gathering, the true boundaries of the law were challenged after 11 September 2001. As a result of the attacks on America, Congress passed the USA Patriot Act of 2001.[117] In addition to sweeping changes in Presidential authority, the Patriot Act included several changes in *FISA*. For instance, the law allowed for "roving" intelligence, thus allowing multi-point wiretap

---

[113]*Foreign Intelligence Surveillance Act of 1978*, Public Law 95-511, *U.S. Statutes at Large* 92 (1978): 1738, codified at *U.S. Code* 50 (2008), §§ 1801-1811. For additional history on FISA, see infra chapter 4.

[114]Jimmy Carter, *Foreign Intelligence Surveillance Act of 1978, Statement on Signing S. 1566 Into Law*, in *Public Papers of the Presidents of the United States: Jimmy Carter, 1978, Vol. 2* (Washington, DC: Government Printing Office, 1979), 1853.

[115]*Foreign Intelligence Surveillance Act of 1978*, §§ 1801-1811.

[116]Ibid.

[117]*USA Patriot Act*, 272.

warrants targeted to individuals, rather than specific locations or telephone numbers.[118] In addition, the Patriot Act allowed for greater information sharing between criminal investigators and the Director of National Intelligence.[119] Specifically, the Act authorizes law enforcement officials to disclose certain foreign intelligence information uncovered during a criminal investigation or even a secret grand jury.[120]

At approximately the same time as the Patriot Act, President Bush signed a classified executive order authorizing the National Security Agency (NSA), without FISA warrants, "to intercept international communications of people with known links to al Qaeda and related terrorist organizations."[121] In 2005, the *New York Times* reported the existence of this secret program, thus beginning a public dialogue over the viability of the *FISA* restrictions in a post-11 September intelligence environment.[122] As a result, Congress made several additional amendments to *FISA*. In 2007, the President signed the *Protect America Act*, a temporary measure that authorized the Attorney General and the

---

[118]Ibid., § 1805(c)(2)(B).

[119]Charles Doyle, CRS Report for Congress, *The USA Patriot Act: A Legal Analysis* (Washington, DC: Government Printing Office, 2002), 23. Although past FISA provisions had defined "foreign power" to include "a group engaged in international terrorism or activities in preparation thereof," the *Patriot Act* reinforces the power to conduct surveillance against terrorism syndicates, like al-Qaeda, that are not directly tied to foreign governments. Ibid.

[120]Ibid. The law does, however, require the Department of Justice to confidentially notify the court of any grand jury disclosures to intelligence officials. Ibid.

[121]The White House, "President's Radio Address," 17 December 2005, http://georgewbush-whitehouse.archives.gov/news/releases/2005/12/ 20051217.html (accessed 21 January 2010).

[122]James Risen, and Eric Lichtblau, "Bush Lets U.S. Spy on Callers Without Courts," *New York Times*, 16 December 2005.

Director of National Intelligence to approve surveillance without a court order.[123] Meanwhile, the FISA court was given the power to oversee the government's surveillance procedures.[124] Congress included a sunset provision in the law which returned *FISA* to the status quo ante after six months.

In an effort to effect more permanent change to *FISA*, Congress passed the *FISA Amendments Act of 2008*.[125] The amendments included major changes to the procedures articulated in the original *FISA*. For example, the Amendments Act grants immunity to telecommunications companies that complied with certain intelligence agency wiretapping requests.[126] In addition, the Act extends the period for warrantless wiretapping under emergency circumstances from forty-eight hours to seven days.[127] Finally, the act provides new protections to American citizens abroad that were not in the original act.[128] While the expanded powers under the *FISA Amendments Act* were

[123]*Protect America Act of 2007*, Public Law 110-55, *U.S. Statutes at Large* 121 (2007): 552; Bill Moyers Journal, "The Church Committee and FISA."

[124]The White House, "Fact Sheet: The Protect America Act of 2007," 6 August 2007, http://georgewbush-whitehouse.archives.gov/news/releases/2007/08/20070806-5.html (accessed 21 January 2010).

[125]*Foreign Intelligence Surveillance Act of 1978 Amendments Act of 2008*, Public Law 110-261, *U.S. Statutes at Large* 122 (2008): 2436.

[126]Erich Lichtblau, "Senate Approves Bill to Broaden Wiretap Powers," *New York Times*, 10 July 2008.

[127]Ibid.

[128]"What is in the New Intelligence Bill," *CNN.com*, 9 July 2008, http://www.cnn.com/2008/POLITICS/07/09/fisa.explainer/index.html?iref=allsearch (accessed 22 April 2010).

controversial, many lawmakers believe the changes were necessary to modernize *FISA* and adequately protect the United States.

Intelligence Oversight-Executive Branch

In addition to *FISA*, the Church Report also recommended comprehensive intelligence oversight architecture. In essence, the genesis for intelligence oversight was the perceived violations of the PCA by Army Intelligence. As a result, President Ford issued an executive order that established "effective oversight to assure compliance with law in the management and direction of intelligence agencies and departments of the national government."[129] This initial executive order laid the foundation for the Department of Defense's intelligence oversight program.[130] Today, the Assistant to the Secretary of Defense for Intelligence Oversight (ATSD(IO)) "is responsible to the Secretary of Defense for the independent oversight of all intelligence, counterintelligence, and intelligence-related activities in the Department of Defense."[131] In addition, the ATSD(IO) is responsible for administering the DoD Intelligence Oversight Program. This program has been furthered expanded to make intelligence oversight rules applicable to the National Guard, effectively limiting the various States'

---

[129]Executive Order 11,905, *U.S. Congressional and Administrative News*, vol 5, (1977): 7703

[130]Assistant to the Secretary of Defense for Intelligence Oversight, "Mission and History: Assistant to the Secretary of Defense (Intelligence Oversight)," http://atsdio.defense.gov/ (accessed 22 April 2010).

[131]Ibid; Department of Defense, Directive 5148.11, "Assistant to the Secretary of Defense for Intelligence Oversight" (Washington, DC: Government Printing Office, 21 May 2004).

National Guard ability to collect domestic intelligence in the same manner as federal forces.[132]

The DoD Intelligence Oversight Program contains several initiatives to ensure intelligence collection complies with applicable laws. The program includes three main categories: "The orientation and training of all intelligence personnel in intelligence oversight concepts; [a]n internal inspection program, and; [a] channel for the reporting of questionable or improper intelligence activities to the ATSD (IO) and the DoD General Counsel, who are responsible for informing the Secretary and Deputy Secretary of Defense."[133] Based on these three main categories, all subordinate intelligence agencies within the Department of Defense, in addition to the military branches, have developed intelligence oversight programs.[134]

---

[132]Department of the Army and the Air Force, National Guard Bureau, Memorandum, "NGB Policy for Handling of U.S. Persons Information," 18 June 2008; Department of the Navy, Marine Corps Order 3800.2B, "Oversight of Intelligence Activities," 20 April 2004.

[133]Assistant to the Secretary of Defense (Intelligence Oversight), "Mission and History: Assistant to the Secretary of Defense (Intelligence Oversight)."

[134]Executive Order no. 12,333: 200; Executive Order no. 13,355: 218; and Executive Order 13,470; 45325; Chairman of the Joint Chiefs of Staff, Instruction 5901.01B, *Joint Staff Inspector General Responsibilities, Procedures, and Oversight Functions*, 11 July 2008; Department of the Army, Regulation 381-10, *U.S. Army Intelligence Activities* (Washington, DC: Government Printing Office, 3 May 2007), chapter 15; Department of the Air Force, Instruction 14-104, *Oversight of Intelligence Activities* (Washington, DC: Government Printing Office, 16 April 2007); Department of the Army and the Air Force, National Guard Bureau, Memorandum, "NGB Policy for Handling of U.S. Persons Information"; Department of the Navy, Marine Corps Order 3800.2B; Department of the Navy, Instruction 3820.3E, "Oversight of Intelligence Activities within the Navy (DON)," 21 September 2005; National Geospatial Intelligence Agency, Instruction 8900.4R5, *NGA Instruction for Intelligence Oversight*, 30 March 2006.

One of the most important functions of the intelligence oversight program is to encourage government employees to report suspicious activity when they see it. In so doing, the government enlists the assistance of the thousands of government employees who are in the best position to identify and report suspicious activity. In order to encourage such reporting, the ATSD(IO) makes clear that "[t]hose reporting a questionable intelligence activity are protected from reprisal or adverse actions associated with this reporting by anyone in their entire chain of command."[135] As a result of intelligence oversight programs, many suspicious intelligence incidents have been reported and investigated, thereby preventing many of the abuses identified by the Church Report.

Intelligence Oversight--Congress

In addition to the Executive Branch's intelligence oversight program, Congress also has a robust intelligence oversight program. Approximately one year after the establishment of the CIA, Congressional members considered establishing a joint committee on intelligence.[136] Although a joint committee was not established, several changes did occur, "including, most importantly, the creation of parallel Select Committees on Intelligence in both chambers."[137] These select committees are extremely

---

[135]Assistant to the Secretary of Defense (Intelligence Oversight), "Reporting of Intelligence Oversight (IO) Questionable Activities," http://atsdio.defense.gov/ documents/quickref.html (accessed 20 January 2010).

[136]Fredrick M. Kaiser, CRS Report for Congress, *Congressional Oversight of Intelligence: Current Structure and Alternatives* (Washington, DC: Government Printing Office, 2008), 1.

[137]Ibid.

influential, with the power to make recommendations on appropriations for the various intelligence agencies. Both of the committees have "broad jurisdiction over the intelligence community and report authorizations and other legislation for consideration by their respective chambers."[138] Given their wide scope, the select committees on intelligence play a large role in intelligence policy and structure.

Despite their identical functions, Senate and House Select Committees on Intelligence are run differently. For instance, the House committee requires all members to swear not to disclose classified information obtained by the committee.[139] Surprisingly, the Senate does not have a similar procedure for its members. In addition, the size of the panels varies greatly, with the House panel composed of 21 members and the Senate panel composed of 15.[140] Finally, the composition of the panels varies from the House to the Senate in terms of "tenure, and other membership features, including partisan composition and leadership arrangements."[141]

In addition to administrative inconsistencies between the two committees, Congress has identified deficiencies in the ability to oversee intelligence with two parallel committees. In fact, "[t]he 9/11 Commission's report, released in 2004, notably concluded that congressional oversight of intelligence was 'dysfunctional' and recommended either a merger of appropriations and authorization powers into each select

---

[138]Ibid., 3.

[139]Ibid., 4.

[140]Ibid.

[141]Ibid.

committee or the creation of a Joint Committee on Intelligence."[142] Since the 11

September attacks, both committees have made changes in their structure, yet they

continue to resist standardization or consolidation of the two committees.[143]

The considerable efforts in intelligence oversight by both the Executive and

Legislative Branches are due in large part to the PCA violations stemming from Post-

Vietnam era Army Intelligence activities. As a result, these rules are a constant reminder

of the PCA restrictions imposed on federal military forces.

Conclusion

This section has explored the existing interpretations and literature regarding

domestic intelligence, the PCA, and the emergence of laws designed to prevent

intelligence abuses. The next section, research methodology, will describe how these

sources will serve as the foundation for an analysis of how PCA effects information

sharing initiatives.

---

[142]U.S. National Commission on Terrorist Attacks Upon the United States, 420.

[143]Kaiser, 1.

CHAPTER 3

RESEARCH METHODOLOGY

Overview

The qualitative research methodology was used in this thesis. While qualitative research is difficult to define, a common characteristic of qualitative research is that it allows the researcher to "see and understand the context within which decisions and actions take place."[144] Such an understanding of the context surrounding information sharing policy is crucial to framing the true problem in this thesis. As discussed in chapter 2, many of the information sharing initiatives were developed in haste and in direct reaction to the 11 September attacks. Similarly, many Americans have deeply emotional reactions to federal military forces acting as domestic law enforcement, thereby directly influencing the government's interpretation and application of the PCA. Without this greater contextual understanding of policies related to information sharing and the PCA, this research would miss a fundamental key to resolving the research question.

Although qualitative research encompasses a myriad of different methods, the two primary methods relied on in this thesis will be documentary analysis and case study comparison. These methods are particularly useful because they allow the research to be

---

[144]Michael D. Myers, *Qualitative Research in Business and Management* (Los Angeles: SAGE Publications, 2009), 5.

conducted in a "natural setting."[145] In other words, the data provided comes from its own

setting, rather than being generated specifically for this thesis. This "real world" context

is particularly helpful in the study of homeland security, where personal interactions

often result in enduring government policies.[146]

The first research method, documentary analysis, involves reviewing existing

documents to obtain the substantive information contained in them, as well as the subtext

that can be revealed by looking at the documents in the context of other documents and

actions.[147] For instance, much of the legislation that will be analyzed in this thesis

originated as Presidential Executive Orders, and these orders provide background

regarding the need and true purpose for the legislation. In addition, contemporaneous

media coverage will add additional background that reflects the public's view of the laws.

Exploring how the various documents researched in this thesis interrelate is crucial to

developing a deeper understanding of the problem.

The second research method used in this thesis is comparative case study. A case

study is a "strategy of research that aims to understand social phenomena within a single

or small number of naturally occurring settings."[148] Case studies give the researcher the

---

[145]Jane Ritchie, "The Applications of Qualitative Methods to Social Research," in *Qualitative Research Practice: A Guide for Social Science Students and Researchers*, ed. Jane Ritchie and Jane Lewis (London: SAGE Publications, 2003), 34.

[146]Ibid.

[147]Ibid., 35.

[148]Michael Bloor and Fiona Wood, *Keywords in Qualitative Methods: A Vocabulary of Research Concepts* (London: SAGE Publications, 2006), 27.

ability to apply abstract theory to a specific, concrete scenario and obtain a better understanding of how the theory works in practice.

In this thesis, the case studies will illustrate three examples of DoD information sharing and explore whether they violated the PCA. Rather than focusing on the viewpoint of an individual, these case studies focus on the information-sharing process. They also represent developments in law and social attitudes regarding civil-military relations over a period of ninety years. These case studies were chosen because the view of one participant would not provide a "holistic, comprehensive, and contextualized" understanding of the research issue.[149] However, by using process-based case studies, the "integration of different perspectives on the context or interaction" will provide the depth necessary to understand the research issue.[150] The thesis will then compare the three case studies, drawing on similarities and inconsistencies, in order to develop a better understanding of the theory.

One of the considerable dangers of using the case study methodology is the problem of "generalization to a larger population."[151] Although a case study can be illustrative of a widespread phenomenon, too much generalization could lead to a faulty theory that only applies under certain specific conditions. In this thesis, the dangers inherent in generalization will be mitigated by comparing three cases, instead of one.

---

[149]Jane Lewis, "Design Issues," in *Qualitative Research Practice: A Guide for Social Science Students and Researchers*, ed. Jane Ritchie and Jane Lewis (London: SAGE Publications, 2003), 52.

[150]Ibid.

[151]Bloor and Wood, 29.

These cases represent developments in domestic intelligence over the course of ninety years, rather than concentrating on only recent developments. In addition, the case studies selected are representative of the types of information-sharing initiatives undertaken by DoD on a routine basis instead of unique situations unlikely to be encountered again. Finally, all of the case studies are similar situations involving the same entities and relationships, thereby reducing the number of variables amongst the cases. Given these safeguards, the case studies in this thesis are an illuminating and sound research method.

Both the documentary analysis and case study methods used in this thesis serve to reinforce each other. This redundancy, often called triangulation, is defined as "the systematic comparison of findings on the same research topic generated by different research methods."[152] In this thesis, the case studies and documentary analysis will provide alternate views of the same research issue, thereby providing a richer analysis of the research issue.

Research Format

The research format for this thesis mirrors the scientific method.[153] It includes: problem identification, hypothesis development, source material collection and classification, fact organization, conclusion formation, presenting research in an organized form.[154] Both fact organization and presenting research in an organized form

---

[152]Ibid.

[153]For a good example of the scientific research method format, see John A. Nagl, "Asymmetric Threats to U.S. National Security to the Year 2010" (Master's thesis, Command and General Staff College, 2001).

[154]Ibid., 181.

are implicit in the structure of this thesis, and therefore are not detailed in the discussion that follows.

Problem Identification

In this thesis, the central research question is: Is the PCA inhibiting the sharing of intelligence information between DoD and state and local law enforcement?

Evaluation Criteria

Whether the PCA is "inhibiting" DoD information sharing will be evaluated based on three criteria. First, does the actual PCA criminal statute, as written, inhibit the sharing of information? Secondly, do Government interpretations of PCA restrictions, and the resulting policies and decisions that stem from these interpretations (like intelligence oversight), inhibit DoD information sharing? Finally, does public sentiment regarding the PCA and civil-military relations inhibit DoD information sharing?

Whether inhibitions resulting from the PCA are "necessary" will be evaluated based on three criteria. First, do the limitations preserve the image of the military as subordinate to civil authority and perpetuate the military as a trusted government institution? Second, are the restrictions necessary given DoD's resources? Finally, are the restrictions necessary given DoD's training? Chapter 4 will explore all of these criteria to answer the ultimate thesis question posed.

Development of a Hypothesis

I will test the following hypotheses: First, the PCA is inhibiting DoD intelligence information sharing efforts. Secondly, these restrictions are necessary in light of the greatly expanded role DoD plays in homeland security and America's beliefs regarding civil-military relations.

Source Material Collection and Classification

The amount of information available on this subject can be overwhelming. As a result, after significant collection efforts, the materials were divided into two main sub-components: primary source documents and secondary sources. For primary sources, the multitude of Presidential Executive Orders were particularly helpful in providing context for the various information-sharing entities formed after the attacks of 11 September. For secondary sources, the many books on the national intelligence structure were particularly helpful.

After dividing the sources into primary and secondary, the sources were further sub-divided by theme: intelligence-related materials, information-sharing materials, and PCA-related materials. The PCA-related materials included several helpful law review articles dealing with the evolution of the PCA, along with Congressional Research Service reports that detail the laws applicability in a post-11 September 2001 environment. The literature review sub-sections mirror the theme divisions listed above.

Conclusion Formation

Based on the analysis provided in chapter 4, the conclusion will present confirmatory or falsify evidence of the hypothesis. The case studies and document analysis used in chapters 2 and 4 will provide an answer. In evaluating the research, primary sources received greater weight than secondary sources. Finally, within secondary sources, books and law review articles received greater weight than media coverage. As discussed previously, the case studies were used to illustrate the theories espoused in the documentary analysis. The case studies are not necessarily an accurate representation of the greater population. However, as major occurrences of military involvement with domestic intelligence, they may be considered as indicative of other cases in the population.[155] With multiple research methods, plentiful sources, and disciplined analysis, the conclusion will represent an unbiased answer to the research question.

---

[155]Richard E. Berkebile, interviewed by author, Fort Leavenworth, Kansas, 4 May 2010.

CHAPTER 4

ANALYSIS

After outlining the current U.S. intelligence structure, the extensive history of the PCA, and the central role that information sharing now plays in the intelligence community in chapters 1 and 2, this chapter will explore the nature and extent of the PCA's impact on information-sharing. The first section will address the rather basic question of whether the DoD must play a role in domestic intelligence information-sharing. This section will address the internal and external customers that DoD services through their domestic intelligence programs. In addition, this section will explore the resources currently allocated to DoD and the implications of moving them to another Executive Agency.

The second section will explore the nature of the PCA restrictions on DoD domestic intelligence gathering, both actual constraints dictated by the law, as well as instances in which federal authorities have made policy determinations that restricted intelligence gathering. This section will consist of three case studies in which federal forces participated in domestic intelligence gathering: War Plans White, Vietnam-era intelligence, and Post-11 September intelligence. These case studies serve to illustrate the practical implications of applying the PCA to DoD intelligence. Through these case studies, the section will define the actual parameters of the PCA, as well as the various interpretations that have guided DoD domestic intelligence gathering over the years.

Finally, having established that the PCA does inhibit DoD information-sharing, the final section will explore whether these restrictions are appropriate in light of current threats to the homeland and America's current beliefs regarding civil-military relations.

By assessing the true nature of the PCA, how it impacts DoD information-sharing, and whether such restrictions are appropriate, this chapter will answer the central question of whether the PCA inhibits DoD information-sharing efforts.

Must the DoD Continue to Participate in Domestic Intelligence Information-Sharing?

As discussed in chapter 1, the DoD controls the vast majority of the U.S. intelligence budget. Through a complex system of agencies, the DoD satisfies the intelligence requirements of the military, national leaders, and foreign partner countries. Although the primary function of these intelligence agencies is to collect foreign intelligence, DoD has experienced a dramatic and necessary increase in domestic intelligence gathering. The reason for this increase is threefold. First, the attacks of 11 September have created a large internal demand for domestic intelligence. In addition to increased foreign intelligence, DoD relies on domestic intelligence in order to "connect the dots" that reveal a potential terrorist attack against military installations or critical infrastructure. If DoD were to confine its intelligence gathering to solely foreign intelligence, it would compromise efforts to identify key terrorist activities in the United States that may expose a terrorist plot against designated DoD interests.

The second reason for the increase is the vast number of "new customers" DoD must now support. Along with DHS and many other federal agencies, state and local law enforcement has come to rely on DoD's significant intelligence capabilities to collect terrorism-related information. The final reason for the increase in DoD domestic intelligence gathering is perhaps the most obvious--DoD controls the vast majority of the federal government's intelligence budget. With this control comes the corresponding obligation to provide assistance to agencies that do not possess the same level of intelligence capability. The remainder of this subsection will address each of these justifications for DoD domestic intelligence gathering.

DoD's Internal Demand for Domestic Intelligence

The DoD is the lead agency for homeland defense, focusing on protecting the homeland from external threats. Consequently, the majority of DoD's intelligence assets were traditionally focused on collecting and analyzing foreign intelligence. The 11 September attacks exposed seams in the foreign and domestic intelligence fabric that caused a reevaluation of intelligence duties. Consequently, DoD's domestic intelligence mission has steadily expanded over the past nine years.

In November 2001, the Army Deputy Chief of Staff for Intelligence issued guidance on the collection of domestic intelligence gathering.[156] In the memorandum, he characterized the global terror network as one in which operatives exist within, as well as outside, the United States. The memorandum goes on to announce the "pivotal role" Army Military Intelligence would play in the global fight.[157] He specifically addressed the role of the military in collecting domestic intelligence, stating: "Contrary to popular belief, there is no absolute ban on intelligence components collecting U.S. person

---

[156]Lieutenant General Robert W. Noonan, Department of the Army, Memorandum, "Collecting Information on U.S. Persons," 5 November 2001.

[157]Ibid.

information."[158] This memorandum is representative of the considerable efforts of the

DoD over the next several years to clarify their role in domestic intelligence gathering.

The DoD's intelligence capability greatly increased with the creation of

NORTHCOM in 2002, and this rapid expansion led to significant management

challenges.[159] In a 2002 interview, General (GEN) Ralph Eberhart, the Commander of

NORTHCOM, acknowledged that the command would compile and analyze domestic

intelligence, but "we are not going to be out there spying on people trying to get

information on people . . . that's not our mission."[160] The primary mission would be to

analyze domestic intelligence to uncover threats to military forces and installations. To

accomplish this intelligence mission, NORTHCOM relied on a robust internal

intelligence directorate, initially estimated by GEN Eberhart at approximately 150

analysts, along with the Counterintelligence Field Activity (CIFA) created in late

---

[158]Ibid.

[159]In addition to the creation of NORTHCOM, the President established a reaction force in the event of a future domestic disaster. Called a "chemical, biological, radiological and high-yield explosive (CBRNE) consequence management response force (CCMRF)," the capability allows NORTHCOM to send an "initial response force" in reaction to a domestic incident. United States Northern Command, "U.S. Northern Command Gains Dedicated Response Force," 30 September 2008, http://www.northcom.mil/News/2008/093008.html (accessed 19 April 2010). The introduction of a dedicated military force to be used within the United States has been met with widespread skepticism in the press. Larry Shaughnessy, "Army Combat Unit to Deploy within U.S.," *CNN.com*, 3 October 2008, http://edition.cnn.com/2008/US/10/03/army.unit/index.html (accessed 19 April 2010).

[160]PBS Online NewsHour, "An Online NewsHour Report: Air Force General Ralph Eberhart," Public Broadcasting System, 27 September 2002, http://www.pbs.org/newshour/terrorism/ata/Eberhart.html (accessed 20 April 2010).

2002.[161] By 2005, NORTHCOM employed 290 intelligence analysts, in addition to the undisclosed number employed by CIFA.[162]

The primary mission of CIFA was to "develop and manage DoD Counterintelligence (CI) programs and functions that support the protection of the department."[163] In support of this effort, CIFA managed the TALON system, an Internet database that allowed civilians and military members to report suspicious activity that might threaten the military.[164] This system was soon supplemented by the Joint Protection Enterprise Network (JPEN), a commercially available database that was adapted to military use.[165] The system allowed various agencies to share information related to force protection and antiterrorism with the DoD. At the time of its unveiling, the Chairman of the Joint Chiefs, GEN Myers, hailed it as "too good to be true. . . . The beauty of it is, you can link anybody, and everybody, and everybody can put in data."[166]

---

[161]Ibid.

[162]Walter Pincus, "Pentagon Expanding Its Domestic Surveillance Activity," *The Washington Post*, 27 November 2005.

[163]Department of Defense, Directive 5105.67, "Department of Defense Counterintelligence Field Activity (DoD CIFA)" (Washington, DC: Government Printing Office, 19 February 2002), par. 3.

[164]Lisa Myers, et al., "Is the Pentagon Spying on Americans?," *MSNBC.com*, 14 December 2005, http://www.msnbc.msn.com/id/10454316/ (accessed 20 April 2010).

[165]United States Northern Command, News Release, "JPEN Shares Antiterrorism Information Across Nation," 3 March 2004, http://www.northcom.mil/News/2004/030304.html (accessed 22 April 2010).

[166]Ibid.

Unfortunately, GEN Myers' assessment that it was too good to be true would actually prove prophetic.

Just three years after unveiling CIFA, it soon became perceived as an organization that was gathering and retaining information on innocent U.S. civilians. In late 2005, a series of news article publicized the program and criticized the military's foray into widespread domestic intelligence gathering.[167] In the articles, the agency was accused of using TALON and JPEN to collect and disseminate information related to war protesters.[168] In 2007, the DoD closed the TALON database, and a year later, both CIFA and JPEN were closed because of an intelligence streamlining effort by Secretary of Defense Robert Gates.[169] However, the CIFA resources were transferred to the newly created Defense Counterintelligence and Human Intelligence Center (DCHIC), which is under the direction of the DIA, rather than NORTHCOM.[170] Although the official reason for the move was related to efficiency, a secondary motivation was likely a desire to

---

[167]Myers, et al., "Is the Pentagon Spying on Americans?"

[168]Robert Block and Gary Fields, "Is Military Creeping Into Domestic Spying and Enforcement?," *Wall Street Journal*, 9 March 2004; Samantha Henig, "Pentagon Surveillance of Student Groups Extended to Scrutinizing E-mail," *The Chronicle of Higher Education* 52, no. 46 (21 July 2006): A.21.

[169]Robert Burns, "Pentagon Will Close Antiterror Database," *The Star-Ledger* (Newark, NJ), 22 August 2007; Department of Defense, News Release, "DoD Activates Defense Counterintelligence and Human Intelligence Center," 4 August 2008, http://www.defense.gov/releases/release.aspx?releaseid=12106 (accessed 22 April 2010).

[170]Department of Defense, News Release, "DoD Activates Defense Counterintelligence and Human Intelligence Center."

distance domestic intelligence from the newly-created NORTHCOM.[171] In addition,

recent revisions to FM 2-22.2, *Counterintelligence*, emphasize that "Because Army CI

authority is narrowly focused, the role of CI in domestic operations is very limited."[172]

Despite the reduction of NORTHCOM's domestic intelligence capability, the

need for domestic intelligence related to force protection has increased.[173] This need for

domestic intelligence was highlighted by the tragedy at Fort Hood, Texas in 2009, in

which an Army major shot and killed thirteen people.[174] In the subsequent investigation,

the committee identified faulty force protection measures as one of the lessons learned

from the incident. Specifically, the committee found that information-sharing efforts

---

[171]Such was the case with another popular DoD database. In 2001, The DIA
created the Joint Regional Information Exchange System (JRIES), an online database
designed to exchange DoD information with local law enforcement. In 2003, the database
was transferred from DoD to DHS control. Jordan Debree and Lee Wang, "Frontline: The
Enemy Within: Defending the Home Front: The Military's New Role," Public
Broadcasting System, http://www.pbs.org/wgbh/pages/frontline/enemywithin
/reality/military/html (accessed 22 April 2010). According to DHS, the reason for this
transfer was DIA's concern "that managing JRIES to support domestic intelligence
activities conflicted with its military intelligence role." Department of Homeland
Security, Office of the Inspector General, *Homeland Security Information Network Could
Support Information Sharing More Effectively* (Washington, DC: Government Printing
Office, June 2006), 7.

[172]Department of the Army, FM 2-22.2, *Counterintelligence*, 3-6.

[173]As the Geographic Combatant Command responsible for the United States,
NORTHCOM is responsible for the force protection of U.S.-based Soldiers. Department
of Defense, *Unified Command Plan* (Washington, DC: Government Printing Office,
2008), cited in Department of Defense, *Report of the DoD Independent Review,
Protecting the Force: Lessons from Fort Hood* (Washington, DC: Government Printing
Office, January 2010).

[174]Department of Defense, *Report of the DoD Independent Review, Protecting the
Force: Lessons from Fort Hood*, 27-29.

needed improvement, particularly communication between DoD and Joint Terrorism

Task Forces (JTTF).[175]

The shortfall identified by those investigating the Fort Hood Shooting was further

exacerbated by the lack of a central database to record force protection threats. Since the

deactivation of TALON, the "Department of Defense does not have direct access to a

force protection threat reporting system for suspicious incident activity reports."[176] The

Guardian System, an FBI-managed database that now houses force protection related

intelligence, is the only database with the capability for DoD to share information with

other agencies.[177] Finally, with no real-time information sharing procedures, other

military installations learned of the incident from news media reports. As the report

correctly points out, had the Fort Hood shooting been part of a multi-installation attack,

other installations would have been ill-prepared to defend against the attack.[178] Just three

years after the dismantling of NORTHCOM's domestic intelligence databases, the Fort

Hood incident highlights, with frightening clarity, the importance of DoD's internal

domestic intelligence requirements.

---

[175]Ibid., 28. A Joint Terrorism Task Force (JTTF) is a cell of representatives from various federal, state and local agencies, led by the Department of Justice and the FBI, designed to combine resources and share information. Department of Justice, "Joint Terrorism Task Force," http://www.justice.gov/jttf/ (accessed 22 April 2010).

[176]Ibid., 29.

[177]Ibid., 29. The eGuardian system, a new unclassified version of the Guardian database, has recently been unveiled, but that system is also controlled by the FBI. Ibid.

[178]Ibid., 30.

DoD's New External Intelligence Customers

While DoD serves as the lead agency for homeland defense, it also supports DHS in fulfilling its role as lead agency for homeland security. After DHS was established, leaders realized that the lifeblood of the organization would be foreign and domestic intelligence. In recognition of this, the President tasked many federal agencies with providing intelligence support to the department.[179] In particular, DoD became a crucial DHS partner, with one Congressional report stating that "DoD intelligence, counterintelligence, and law enforcement organizations will be an integral part of the national architecture supporting homeland security-related intelligence production and dissemination."[180] This prediction has proven correct, as DHS continues to rely on the considerable assets of DoD to fulfill domestic intelligence needs.

When DHS was created, it did not receive funding for independent intelligence collection capabilities.[181] Instead, the legislation created a DHS intelligence fusion center and directed the DoD to provide liaisons to the center. As a result, the DoD established the Assistant Secretary of Defense for Homeland Defense who is responsible for coordinating efforts between the DoD and DHS.[182] Through a series of cooperative

---

[179]Department of Defense, Defense Study and Report to Congress, *The DoD Role in Homeland Security* (Washington, DC: Government Printing Office, July 2003), 12.

[180]Ibid., 12-13.

[181]Steve Bowman, CRS Report for Congress, *Homeland Security: The Department of Defense's Role* (Washington, DC: Government Printing Office, 2003), 2.

[182]Ibid. The position has since been renamed "Assistant Secretary of Defense for Homeland Defense and Americas' Security Affairs," with the additional duty of supervision of "Western Hemisphere security affairs for the Department of Defense." Department of Defense, "Defense.gov Biographies: Paul N. Stockton,"

agreements, the DoD continues to provide significant intelligence information to DHS. The DoD's subordinate intelligence agencies, such as the National Geospatial Intelligence Agency (NGA) and the National Reconnaissance Office (NRO), leverage their significant assets in order to support homeland security efforts.

This cooperation has come at considerable cost to the DoD in terms of money, manpower, and reputation, however. As the requests for domestic intelligence increase, gaps in intelligence coverage become apparent. For instance, although CIFA's original mission was to provide intelligence on potential force protection threats, that mission soon expanded to cover the overwhelming demand for additional domestic intelligence.[183] This in turn led to greater reliance on centralized databases to store and share the intelligence with DHS and other agencies. Because of the extraordinary volume of information being generated, the DoD began to rely on data-mining, a process that uses statistical analysis to sift through large amounts of data to expose patterns or links not previously discovered.[184] As a result, data-mining became a growth industry, and by 2004, the federal government had 199 data-mining systems, with 14 related to counterintelligence.[185] Among the databases were several DoD data-mining programs designed to satisfy intelligence requests.

---

http://www.defense.gov/bios/ biographydetail.aspx?biographyid=206 (accessed 22 April 2010).

[183]Richard A. Posner, Column, "Our Domestic Intelligence Crisis," *The Washington Post*, 21 December 2005.

[184]Frederick A.O. Schwarz, Jr. and Aziz Z. Huq, *Unchecked and Unbalanced: Presidential Power in a Time of Terror* (New York: The New Press, 2007), 129.

[185]Ibid.

This rapid expansion of domestic intelligence gathering was a direct result of the DoD's effort to satisfy its external customers' requests. What started as a primarily defensive domestic intelligence gathering endeavor focused on force protection, quickly ballooned into offensive intelligence gathering on more attenuated subjects.[186] As discussed previously, the rapid proliferation of domestic intelligence gathering by the DoD was met with widespread skepticism in the media and in Congress.[187] In effect, the DoD bore the brunt of criticism for what amounted to identifying and responding to the internal and external requests of its customers. Despite the recent realignment of DoD intelligence agencies under Defense Secretary Gates, the demand for domestic intelligence by external customers continues to grow. Whether the streamlined agencies will be able to satisfy their customers' domestic intelligence demands remains a question yet to be answered.

DoD Controls the Vast Majority of the Federal Government's Intelligence Budget

The final justification for the DoD's expanded role in domestic intelligence is the fact that they control the majority of the intelligence budget. Last year's intelligence budget was $49.8 Billion, and the DoD used the majority of that allocation to support the

---

[186]Ibid., 133-134.

[187]For example, Ibid. Despite this criticism, some have advocated the expansion of DoD's role in domestic intelligence. Richard A. Posner, *Uncertain Shield: The U.S. Intelligence System in the Throes of Reform* (Lanham: Rowman & Littlefield, 2006); Posner, "Our Domestic Intelligence Crisis."

vast DoD intelligence network.[188] In the months following the 11 September attacks, officials logically leveraged the considerable capabilities of the DoD's existing intelligence infrastructure to launch aggressive counterterrorism efforts. In the years following the attacks, the Department was granted additional authority and funding to build on its existing mature intelligence infrastructure. Now that this structure is in place, it would prove difficult to simply abandon the system in favor of non-DoD agencies.

Some argue that the easiest way to limit DoD domestic intelligence involvement is to reallocate the resources to other Executive agencies. Such reallocations could prove more complex than they appear. First, all of the DoD intelligence agencies that currently conduct domestic intelligence functions serve a critical role within the DoD. For instance, although NORTHCOM shares the domestic intelligence it gathers with other agencies within the department, the primary purpose of collecting that information is, and must be, primarily for force protection or another legitimate military mission. Although the JPEN database was maligned as an attempt to collect intelligence on U.S. citizens, the abandonment of the system proved a mistake. The Fort Hood Shooting findings make clear that the lack of a DoD central force protection database is a major vulnerability.[189]

Another difficulty with rearranging intelligence assets is that often the receiving agency does not have the infrastructure in place to support the new asset. As an example,

---

[188]Director of National Intelligence, News Release, "DNI Releases Budget Figure for 2009 National Intelligence Program," 30 October 2009, http://www.dni.gov/press_releases/20091030_release.pdf (accessed 20 April 2010); Best, 1.

[189]Department of Defense, *Report of the DoD Independent Review, Protecting the Force: Lessons from Fort Hood*, 30.

the JRIES database provided a vital link between federal agencies and state and local law enforcement. However, when the database was transferred to DHS control in response to public criticism, the transfer did not go smoothly.[190] Since DHS has taken over the database, the system has been managed poorly. The DHS's Inspector General argues the system, now renamed Homeland Security Information Network (HSIN), is too unwieldy to be of use to local law enforcement.[191] Much of the blame for this failure is attributable to the lack of internal DHS intelligence assets to manage the system. This example demonstrates the dangers of simply conducting piecemeal transfer of individual intelligence components to non-DoD agencies that lack the requisite intelligence infrastructure to manage the components. Although such transfers satisfy the immediate political concerns, in the long term, they benefit neither the DoD, nor the receiving agency.

Summary: Must DoD Be Involved in Domestic Intelligence?

Based on the discussion above, it is clear that DoD domestic intelligence is necessary, albeit wrought with peril. The internal requirements for domestic intelligence based on force protection and protection of critical infrastructure cannot be outsourced to other agencies. Even with the current substantial DoD domestic intelligence capability, the Fort Hood Shootings exposed fundamental vulnerabilities that justify additional domestic intelligence assets. Furthermore, the symbiotic relationship currently in place

---

[190]Department of Homeland Security, Office of the Inspector General, *Homeland Security Information Network Could Support Information Sharing More Effectively.*

[191]Ibid.

between the DoD, DHS and local law enforcement would be difficult to alter without

causing additional intelligence gaps. Finally, the DoD possesses the intelligence

infrastructure capable of supporting the myriad of intelligence assets needed to maintain

effective domestic situational awareness. As a result, the answer to the secondary

question of whether DoD should and must be involved in domestic intelligence must be

answered in the affirmative.

Is the PCA Restricting DoD Information Sharing?

Having established that DoD involvement in domestic intelligence is necessary,

the next question is whether the PCA is actually restricting the sharing of this domestic

intelligence with state and local law enforcement. In determining the nature of these

restrictions, this section will explore both actual restrictions as articulated in the law, as

well as restrictions that have been emplaced as a matter of policy. In order to illustrate

these restrictions, case studies will be used to apply the law to three real world situations:

Vietnam War-era DoD domestic intelligence activities; the standoff at Wounded Knee,

South Dakota; and the Post-11 September 2001 information-sharing initiatives. These

case studies demonstrate that the current sharing initiatives are just the most recent

chapter in a long history of DoD domestic intelligence activities.

Black Letter Law and Regulation

As discussed in chapter 1, the PCA specifically prohibits the federal military from

conducting domestic law enforcement activities.[192] Since its passage in 1878, the act has

---

[192] *U.S. Code* 18 (2008), § 1385.

been altered little, but clarified frequently. In 1981, for instance, Congress passed

clarifications to the PCA in the form of the *Military Cooperation with Law Enforcement*

Officials Act.[193] In an effort to enable the military to cooperate on the newly declared

War on Drugs,[194] the law contained a specific provision related to the "Use of

Information Collected During Military Operations."[195] This provision allows the DoD to

share intelligence information collected "*during the normal course* [emphasis added] of

military training or operations."[196] Although the provision appears to clearly reinforce the

fundamentals of the Post-11 September 2001 information sharing initiative, some doubt

the domestic intelligence being collected and shared is truly in the normal course of

---

[193]*Military Cooperation with Law Enforcement Officials Act*, Public Law 97-86, §
905, *U.S. Statutes at Large* 95 (1981): 1115, codified as amended at *U.S. Code* 10 (2008):
§§ 371-378.

[194]Sean J. Kealy, "Reexamining the Posse Comitatus Act: Toward a Right to Civil
Law Enforcement," *Yale Law and Policy Review* 21 (Spring 2003): 383.

[195]*U.S. Code* 10 (2008), § 371.

[196]*U.S. Code* 10 (2008), § 371. The entire provision states:

(a) The Secretary of Defense may, in accordance with other applicable
law, provide to Federal, State, or local civilian law enforcement officials any
information collected during the normal course of military training or operations
that may be relevant to a violation of any Federal or State law within the
jurisdiction of such officials.

(b) The needs of civilian law enforcement officials for information shall,
to the maximum extent practicable, be taken into account in the planning and
execution of military training or operations.

(c) The Secretary of Defense shall ensure, to the extent consistent with
national security, that intelligence information held by the Department of Defense
and relevant to drug interdiction or other civilian law enforcement matters is
provided promptly to appropriate civilian law enforcement officials. Ibid.

military operations. In an effort to define the parameters of appropriate "military operations" involving intelligence collection, DoD published clarifying directives. The DoD allows intelligence collection on non-DoD personnel under three circumstances: intelligence related to protection of DoD functions and property; intelligence related to personnel security; and in support of operations related to civil disturbances.[197] The first function relates to the DoD's ability to ensure force protection measures. In such cases, the DoD can collect information related to individuals encouraging subversion of loyalty or encouraging violation of the law; theft of DoD property or damage to facilities; and direct threats to DoD military or civilian personnel. Regarding personnel security, the DoD may collect information related to applicants for admission into the military; DoD civilian applicants, and those seeking access to certain official information. Finally, the Defense Secretary may grant prior authorization to collect information that will help DoD "assist civil authorities in dealing with civil disturbances."[198] Within these three seemingly narrow circumstances, DoD actually collects a significant amount of domestic intelligence information.

Once the information is collected, DoD must analyze it for intelligence value related to these three missions.[199] If the information is not directly related to their mission, DoD must purge it unless it reveals a federal or state legal violation. In such

---

[197]Department of Defense, Directive 5200.27, "Acquisition of Information Concerning Persons and Organizations not Affiliated with the Department of Defense" (Washington, DC: Government Printing Office, 7 January 1980).

[198]Department of Defense, Directive 5200.27.

[199]This review must be conducted within 90 days of receipt. Department of Defense, Directive 5200.27, par. (F)(4).

cases, the DoD agency may refer the information to federal, state, or local law enforcement agencies for additional processing.[200] For information collected and stored by DoD agencies, they have "an affirmative responsibility to share collected and stored information, data, and resulting analysis with" other federal agencies and civilian law enforcement.[201]

This affirmative duty to share information with other agencies makes it even more crucial that DoD confine its intelligence collection to the missions articulated under law. If the DoD improperly obtains information, and then passes it on to other agencies, the intelligence violation could potentially be perpetuated throughout the government. However, guidance in the immediate aftermath of 11 September 2001 did not account for such scenarios. In his guidance to Army Intelligence, the Deputy Chief of Staff for Intelligence made clear that "Army Intelligence may always receive information, if only to determine its intelligence value and whether it can be collected, retained, or disseminated in accordance with governing policy."[202] Although this statement is accurate, it may cause confusion regarding whether improperly obtained information must be disseminated after it comes into DoD's possession.

---

[200]Department of Defense, Directive 5525.5, 8.

[201]Department of Defense, Directive 5240.01, "DoD Intelligence Activities" (Washington, DC: Government Printing Office, 27 August 2007), 2; Jeffrey S. Gorden, U.S. NORTHCOM, Senior Law Enforcement Coordination Officer, interviewed by author, Fort Leavenworth, Kansas, 16 February 2010.

[202]Noonan, 2.

Case Studies

Having defined the parameters of the PCA and DoD's intelligence gathering

mission, the following case studies illustrate the difficulties of applying this black letter

law to real world situations.

War Plans White

The expansion of DoD domestic intelligence operations has been met with

skepticism by the American public since the founding of the country. However, the

modern era of DoD domestic intelligence for the purposes of this analysis dates back to

World War I and War Plans White.[203] In 1917, the Bolsheviks took over control of

Russia, negotiating peace with Germany soon thereafter.[204] After a series of diplomatic

missteps, the Wilson Administration sent Army Expeditionary Forces (AEF) to Russia to

thwart Bolshevik attempts to consolidate power.[205] This intervention was extremely

unpopular among U.S. Socialists, and the government soon feared that the Bolshevik

appeals to laborers to overthrow the capitalist government would lead to anarchy in the

United States. As a result, the Army's Military Intelligence Division (MID) and the

Office of Naval Intelligence soon began recruiting Soldiers, Sailors, and civilian

---

[203]Joan M. Jensen, *Army Surveillance in America: 1775-1980* (New Haven: Yale University Press, 1991), 178.

[204]William Henry Chamberlin, *The Russian Revolution* (New York: The Universal Library, 1965), 2: 389-413.

[205]Neil G. Carey, ed., *Fighting the Bolsheviks: The Russian War Memoir of Private First Class Donald E. Carey, U.S. Army, 1918-1919* (Novato: Presidio Press, 1997).

organizations to begin spying activities.[206] The purpose of this spying was to classify American citizens as loyal, loyal but ill-advised, or disloyal.[207] Through these classifications, the MID could then begin to thwart disloyal activities.

What started as an intelligence-gathering effort by MID soon became the genesis for War Plans White. This contingency plan was designed to suppress "a vast conspiracy to overthrow the government of the United States."[208] Organizers of the revolution would accomplish their aims by seizing the transportation hubs, thereby cutting off food distribution to urban areas. After manufacturing this crisis, the radicals would seize control of the food and distribute it to the population, thereby controlling the local government and garnering the support of the local population.[209] Similar to the Bolshevik Revolution, the Communists would take control of the United States through class warfare.[210] Although this threat was a real fear of many in the United States government, the plan was practically an impossibility given the lack of effective organization and the strength of the existing government.[211] Nonetheless, through War Plans White, the military devised a plan to quell any uprising.

---

[206]Ann Hagedorn, *Savage Peace* (New York: Simon & Schuster, 2007), 25.

[207]Jensen, 179.

[208]Curt Gentry, J. Edgar Hoover: The Man and the Secrets (New York: W.W. Norton & Company, 1991), 77.

[209]Jensen, 190.

[210]Ibid.

[211]Ibid.; *The Church Report*, Book 6, 113.

In an effort to control dissenting groups, the government relied on both the

military and civilian law enforcement to identify and control dissenting groups. The

Army's MID conducted surveillance of individuals with suspected ties to Communist

groups. However, given the perceived pervasiveness of the problem, the Army enlisted

the aid of several civilian volunteer organizations to increase their intelligence-gathering

capabilities.[212] For example, the MID used organizations such as the United Americans

and the American Legion as surrogates to spy on political groups.[213] In some cases, the

American Legion and American Protective League (APL) began to conduct raids on

suspected communist groups, seizing membership rosters, destroying literature, and

assisting in the arrest of leaders.[214] In fact, for a short time, War Plans White called for

the American Legion to act as a group "the army could call upon to maintain law and

order should the necessity exist."[215] These efforts were further supplemented by civilian

law enforcement.

In 1918, J. Edgar Hoover assumed control of the "Radical Division" of the Justice

Department. Through this position, he used the APL, a group of businessmen who agreed

---

[212]Hagedorn, 25. The civilian volunteer organizations included "the Liberty League, the American defense Society, the Home Defense League, the National Security League, the Anti-Yellow dog League, the All-Allied Anti-German League, the Knights of Liberty, the Boy Spies of America, the American Anti-Anarchy Association, and the Sedition Slammers." Ibid.

[213]Hagedorn, 401.

[214]Ibid. In a particularly violent encounter, four Legionnaires were killed in a skirmish with Industrial Workers of the World (IWW) members in Centralia, Washington. Raymond Moley, Jr., *The American Legion Story* (Westport: Greenwood Press, 1966), 97-100.

[215]Jensen, 194.

to collect information on disloyal behavior, to root out the Communist threat.[216] In conjunction with MID, Hoover used APL volunteers to observe and report suspicious activities. In addition, both MID and Hoover urged the volunteers to keep their activities secret because of the potential ramifications of military and civilian involvement in domestic spying.[217]

Despite the military's effort to keep the spying program classified, the public soon uncovered the military's role in intelligence collection and raids on political groups. With the Armistice ending World War I just a week old, MID's leader, Marlborough Churchill, ordered an end to all civilian investigations. As he explained in the memo, "'The emergency no longer exists,' . . . and any 'unfinished disloyalty' cases were to be turned over to the Department of Justice."[218] As a result, MID arranged a cooperative agreement with the Justice Department to transfer many of their intelligence activities to civilian law enforcement. Despite this agreement, however, the MID continued to collect intelligence on U.S. citizens.[219] In fact, even a March 1922 War Department Order that rescinded MID's authority to conduct direct investigations did not end their domestic intelligence activities.[220]

---

[216]Gentry, 71-74; *The Church Report*, Book 6, 98.

[217]*The Church Report*, Book 6, 103; Bruce W. Bidwell, *History of the Military Intelligence Division, Department of the Army General Staff: 1775-1941* (Frederick: University Publications of America, 1986), 276.

[218]Hagedorn, 31.

[219]Bidwell, 277-278.

[220]Jensen, 198.

In the fall of 1922, a MID officer sent a letter to local civilian law enforcement informing them that MID was responsible for conducting "surveillance of all organizations or elements hostile or potentially hostile to the government of this country, or who seek to overthrow the government by violence."[221] After the letter was published in several newspapers throughout the country, the Secretary of War was finally forced to deal with the expanded role of MID in domestic intelligence. In December of 1922, Secretary of War John Weeks significantly curtailed the activities of MID, requiring that they receive special approval from the War Department prior to collecting domestic intelligence other than through the Corps of Intelligence Police.[222] Despite another clear prohibition on domestic intelligence collection, however, the MID, later known as the G2, continued to collect information on political activities in support of its efforts "to maintain an up-to-date emergency plan covering the possible commitment of their troops in local civil disturbances."[223] In short, the same justification that would be used in the 1970s to collect domestic intelligence on U.S. civilians was used throughout the interwar period to collect extensive intelligence on politically active civilians.

Lessons from the War Plans White Era

Although the military structure and laws regarding domestic intelligence have changed significantly since the 1920s, many lessons can be taken from the War Plans White era. First, the public's skepticism regarding military involvement in domestic

---

[221]Bidwell, 279.

[222]Ibid., 278.

[223]Ibid.

intelligence gathering was as strong in the 1920s as it is today. Although initially

authorized to conduct domestic intelligence gathering to protect against wartime

sabotage, the government soon expanded MID's mission to root out political dissent. As

MID's leader made clear at the end of 1919, the wartime "emergency no longer

exist[ed]."[224] However, because of conflicting guidance from within the federal

government, many field agents continued collecting intelligence on civilians for several

more years. In fact, even after the MID's activities were exposed in the press in 1924,

domestic intelligence operations continued throughout the 1930s.[225] Such seemingly

insidious behavior caused both the press and the public to become critical of the

military's involvement in domestic intelligence. These incidents damaged the Army's

reputation to the extent that any information gathering in preparation for domestic

operations was eventually prohibited. As a result of over-zealous intelligence activities,

for a time, the Army lost the ability to even prepare for legitimate domestic missions.

Another lesson illustrated by the War Plans White era is the negative effects of

information sharing. The MID partnered with both federal agencies and civilian

businesses to identify radical groups. Just as today's National Strategy for Information

Sharing calls for a partnership between federal and state authorities and the private

sector,[226] the Army's MID partnered with local government and business leaders to

obtain intelligence. As a result, both federal and state agencies received volumes of

---

[224]Hagedorn, 31.

[225]Jensen, 203-207.

[226]The White House, *National Strategy for Information Sharing*, 11.

intelligence information. However, because the source of the information was often unclear, the accuracy of the information was frequently questionable. Also, the MID used both government and private sector sources as thinly-veiled surrogates to obtain information it would not otherwise be able to collect. Finally, after MID established a symbiotic relationship with these other entities, the Army was unable to curtail their activities because other federal and state authorities had grown to rely on their domestic intelligence capabilities. Although the advantages of information sharing are many, the drawbacks of too much integration can also be significant.

Whenever the military ventures into the collection of intelligence related to political associations, the public becomes wary. As General Pershing's intelligence officer argued at the time of the War Plans White controversy,

> I do not believe that the Army has the right, the knowledge or the facilities for determining what individuals or organizations in America stand for good government and what stand for bad government. . . . The Army cannot condemn individual citizens or groups of citizens because of their political views so long as they come within the provisions of the laws which the army itself is required to enforce.[227]

Despite the protestations of many in the military intelligence community at the time, the military continued to collect significant domestic intelligence on civilians from both ends of the political spectrum.[228] Just as many today believe military domestic intelligence operations should be strictly limited, so too did much of society in the 1920s.

---

[227]Jensen, 202.

[228]Bidwell, 279-288.

Vietnam War-era Domestic Intelligence

The rapid expansion of DoD domestic intelligence has steadily progressed over the past ninety years. Another notable incident involves the Vietnam War era domestic intelligence program started under the Johnson Administration. In the early 1960s, civil unrest in the South related to racial tensions caused the state law enforcement authorities to become overwhelmed. [229] Under the auspices of the Insurrection Statutes, the President deployed U.S. Army troops to quell the riots and restore order. As an articulated exception to the PCA, the troops were able to act as law enforcement. As these deployments increased, DoD leadership realized that the Army's efforts were hampered by a lack of intelligence on the cities they were patrolling.[230] In response, the Army began to collecting intelligence on groups and individuals in order to prepare contingency plans for future riots.

In the years that followed, the civil unrest steadily increased, as did the Army's intelligence efforts. Although the Army was actually deployed only once in the mid-1960s, they continued to be alerted and prepositioned in the event National Guard troops needed assistance.[231] Finally, in 1967, Federal troops were deployed to Detroit to quell widespread riots. After an eight-day operation, the Army conducted an extensive After-Action Report (AAR) in which both Administration and Army leadership identified significant intelligence shortfalls that could jeopardize the safety of troops in future

---

[229] *The Church Report*, Book 3, 795-796.

[230] Ibid., 796.

[231] Ibid.

operations.[232] As the President's representative noted, "In order to overcome the initial unfamiliarity of the Federal troops with the area of operations, it would be desirable if the several continental armies were tasked with reconnoitering the major cities of the United States in which it appears possible that riots may occur."[233] This recommendation was certainly in keeping with how the military normally prepared for operations, and seemed only logical. In fact, the Supreme Court, in a subsequent case related to Army Intelligence, found no issue with such intelligence gathering. As the Court made clear, "No logical argument can be made for compelling the military to use blind force. When force is employed it should be intelligently directed, and this depends upon having reliable information--in time."[234] This reasoning soon led the DoD to not only compile files on organizations and individuals, but also to conduct covert intelligence operations aimed at penetrating anti-war protests.

Despite the sweeping changes in Army intelligence, the expansion of domestic intelligence was at a slower pace than the Administration would have preferred. By January 1968, the Army was being criticized for failing to assume a larger role in domestic intelligence. In words that would be echoed almost forty years later, then-Attorney General Ramsey Clark argued that "'every resource' must be used in the domestic intelligence effort" and the Army needed to start delivering additional, quality

---

[232]Ibid., 795.

[233]Ibid.

[234]Laird v. Tatum, 408 U.S. 1, 5 (1972).

intelligence on civil disturbances.[235] Because of its significant assets, the Army was also viewed as the most capable of providing the intelligence needed for these operations.[236] Finally, by 1967, Army leadership approved the widespread collection of domestic intelligence related to civil unrest. However, the most extensive intelligence collection effort was yet to come.

In April 1968, the assassination of Dr. Martin Luther King, Jr., caused widespread rioting in the United States. Federal forces were deployed in Washington, D.C., Baltimore, and Chicago, and even more cities had federal troops on standby.[237] In the aftermath of this event, the Army took even greater steps to prepare for civil unrest. Army leadership jettisoned their restrictive interpretation of domestic intelligence gathering and authorized collection on all forms of political activity in any city with the potential for riot activity.[238] In a collection plan with sweeping language and few definitions, the Army used 1500 intelligence agents to collect vast quantities of information with little regard for restraints.[239]

The array of information collected by Army Intelligence during this period was stunning. In order to collect the information, Army Intelligence agents expanded efforts

---

[235]*The Church Report*, Book 3, 797.

[236]Ibid. For example, the Army had over 1000 intelligence agents throughout the country, as well as the communications infrastructure required to disseminate intelligence to law enforcement officials. Ibid.

[237]Ibid., 798.

[238]Ibid., 799-800.

[239]Ibid.

to penetrate groups viewed as potential instigators of civil unrest. However, in the absence of clear guidance, intelligence agents infiltrated events such as: the Poor People's March to Washington; a Halloween party for elementary school children at which a local dissident was expected to appear; a conference of priests convened to discuss birth control measures; and the Southern Christian Leadership Conference of 1968.[240] Aside from these incidents, 58 agents infiltrated protests surrounding the Democratic National Convention of 1968, and 107 agents monitored protests surrounding the 1969 Presidential Inauguration.[241] In addition to widespread infiltrations, Army Intelligence agents also posed as members of the news media and conducted fake interviews with protest leaders to obtain intelligence.[242] Although many of the incidents chronicled above were coordinated without prior approval from Army leadership, the widespread employment of these tactics were a result of the vague guidance given to Army Intelligence practitioners at the time.

Some military leaders began to question the Army's expansive role in domestic intelligence by 1968. For instance, Deputy Secretary of Defense Paul Nitzke denied an Army request for additional resources, citing "reservations regarding the extent of Army involvement in domestic intelligence activities."[243] In addition, the Army Under Secretary pushed for redefining domestic intelligence boundaries on the grounds that

---

[240]Ibid., 800-801.

[241]Ibid., 801.

[242]Ibid., 801-802.

[243]Ibid., 804.

expansive intelligence collection was duplicative and wasteful.[244] Finally, in January

1970, Christopher Pyle, a former Army Intelligence officer, published an extensive article

chronicling the Army's domestic intelligence program.[245] The article detailed the

extensive use of undercover agents to penetrate political protests, as well as the

communications infrastructure that allowed the Army to disseminate the information to

all levels of government.[246] Just five months after the article was published, the Army

rescinded its collection plan and ceased collecting intelligence that was not directly

related to a "distinct threat of civil disturbance exceeding the law enforcement

capabilities of local and State authorities."[247] Although Congressional hearings,

significant intelligence reform, and Supreme Court cases followed, the Army put to rest a

domestic intelligence apparatus that had grown out of control.[248]

Pertinent Characteristics of Vietnam-era Domestic Intelligence

Although the breadth and depth of Army domestic intelligence will likely not be

seen again, many lessons can be taken from this era. Although the measures seemed

---

[244]Ibid. Forty years later, the Secretary of Defense would use the same efficiency argument to curtail NORTHCOM's domestic intelligence activity. Department of Defense, News Release, "DoD Activates Defense Counterintelligence and Human Intelligence Center."

[245]Christopher H. Pyle, "CONUS Intelligence: The Army Watches Civilian Politics," *Washington Monthly* (January 1970): 4-16.

[246]Ibid., 6.

[247]*The Church Report*, Book 3, 806.

[248]For additional discussion on intelligence reforms resulting from the *Church Report*, see supra chapter 2.

extreme in retrospect, at the time Army Intelligence agents likely thought they were simply making effective contributions to help control the domestic crisis. In addition, the domestic intelligence initiatives started off clearly within the purview of the Army's mission: to assist in quelling civil unrest. By failing to collect intelligence on the urban centers likely to erupt in violence, the Army would be placing Soldiers at risk.

Among the many principles illustrated in this case study, three stand out: vague definitions and sweeping authority often leads to abuses; the government continues to look to the military to solve problems because of its significant assets; and the government often comes to regret policy determinations made during times of crisis. In the Vietnam-era case study, one of the greatest factors leading to rapid domestic intelligence expansion was the lack of clear guidance. The 2 May 1968 Collection Plan endorsed sweeping expansion of domestic intelligence against ill-defined targets. In sum, the plan "identified as 'dissident elements' the 'civil rights movement' and the 'anti-Vietnam/anti-draft movements,' and stated that they were 'supporting the stated objectives of foreign elements which are detrimental to the USA.'"[249] However, the document fails to define key terms like "dissident elements," leaving Army Intelligence agents to make ill-informed, and often erroneous interpretations.[250]

In addition, the Army was taking its cues from the Department of Justice (DoJ) and other agencies. The DoJ, in turn, relied on vague legal notions in defending domestic intelligence tactics. When questioned about FBI warrantless wiretaps on the telephone

---

[249]*The Church Report*, Book 3, 798.

[250]Ibid.

calls of a group of protestors at the Chicago Democratic Convention, the Department argued that "'Congress cannot tell the President what means he may employ to obtain information he needs to determine the proper deployment of his forces.'"[251] If valid, this legal theory would give the President unchecked power to authorize domestic intelligence as long as it was linked to civil unrest. Such unfettered use of the military to enforce the laws would be a relatively clear violation of the PCA. The vague guidance, coupled with the external pressure the Army was under to deliver domestic intelligence, led to the abuses detailed in this case study.

Another principle illustrated by the Army's expanded role in domestic intelligence was the tendency for an organization with robust assets like the Army to become co-opted for missions outside their purview. The government was extremely concerned about the inability of civilian law enforcement to deal with the frequent civil disturbances throughout the United States. The Army, with a robust security force and large intelligence network, seemed the most suited to respond to this crisis. In fact, the 1200 Army Intelligence agents stationed around the country were perfect for the mission because they "were young and could easily mix with dissident young groups of all races."[252] In addition, the Army was the only agency with the capacity to rapidly disseminate large volumes of intelligence data to other agencies through its teletype network.[253] In light of these unique capabilities, other agencies within the government

---

[251]Pyle, 9.

[252]*The Church Report*, Book 3, 797.

[253]Ibid.

began to pressure the Army to leverage those resources in the fight against dissident groups. However, many of those agencies urging the Army to participate failed to realize the potential for PCA violations when the Army operates outside of its directed mission.

The final lesson that can be drawn from Vietnam-era domestic intelligence is the tendency for the government to make quick decisions in the midst of national crisis without considering the long-term consequences. There is no doubt that the civil unrest of the 1960s was a serious concern for the entire government. The government was reacting to widespread protests and riots that would frequently exceed the capabilities of civilian law enforcement and National Guard Soldiers.[254] In addition, the Army realized the gravity of the situation. During the Detroit riots, Assistant Chief of Staff for Intelligence announced to his staff in the domestic war room: "'Men, get out your counterinsurgency manuals. We have an insurgency on our hands.'"[255] In response to these extraordinary events, the government looked for quick, feasible ways to address the problems. They turned to the Army because it had the requisite resources and infrastructure to respond to the crisis. Rather than building up the capacity in another agency, the Army could respond immediately. However, neither the Army nor the government considered the ramifications of an expanded military role in domestic intelligence. In addition, the government clearly did not consider how the Army's expanded role would be received by the public once it was reported in the press. This tendency to make short-term decisions in the heat of battle without fully considering the long-term consequences is a lesson that

---

[254]Ibid., 794-796.

[255]Pyle, 8.

the government has had to learn repeatedly over the last several years. In fact, all of the principles outlined above are recurrent throughout the three case studies.

Post-11 September 2001 Domestic Intelligence

The final case study in this chapter deals with the actions taken in the wake of the 11 September 2001 attacks. In light of the traumatic events that occurred on that day, the Pentagon was under immense pressure to ensure America was protected from future terrorist attacks. As a result, DoD experienced sweeping reform in the area of intelligence gathering and dissemination, coupled with an infusion of funding to finance these activities. The programs that emerged from this rapid expansion yielded mixed results. This case study will highlight NORTHCOM's creation of CIFA and its accompanying database, JPEN. As the case study reveals, many of the same lessons learned from the Army's Vietnam-era domestic intelligence experience were re-learned approximately forty years later.

Creation of CIFA

As detailed previously in this chapter, CIFA was created in late 2002 in response to the increasing internal demand for information related to terrorism and force protection.[256] Although the number of employees working at CIFA was classified, media reports estimated that in October 2006 over 400 full-time employees and 800 to 900

---

[256]PBS Online NewsHour, "An Online NewsHour Report: Air Force General Ralph Eberhart," Public Broadcasting System, 27 September 2002, http://www.pbs.org/newshour/terrorism/ata/Eberhart.html (accessed 20 April 2010).

contractors were working at CIFA.[257] In addition, the budget of CIFA was substantial, with over $1 billion spent by the organization in less than four years.[258] Although CIFA's primary mission was to cultivate counterintelligence programs designed to enable force protection, CIFA soon expanded its reach with the launch of JPEN. The JPEN program allowed DoD to share information with other federal agencies as well as state and local law enforcement.[259] The TALON Reporting System, which allowed individuals to report suspicious activity targeted at military installations, fed into the JPEN system unverified raw data collected from numerous sources.[260]

TALON Uses

After CIFA received and processed TALON reports, they distributed the information to military installations, federal agencies, and local law enforcement through JTTFs.[261] These raw reports informed entities about potential events that might cause safety risks to DoD employees or damage to DoD property. Over the course of four years, over 13,000 TALON reports were issued.[262] However, because they were raw

---

[257]Pincus, "Pentagon to End Talon Data-Gathering Program."

[258]Ibid.

[259]United States Northern Command, News Release, "JPEN Shares Antiterrorism Information Across Nation," 3 March 2004, http://www.northcom.mil/News/2004/030304.html (accessed 22 April 2010).

[260]Department of Defense Inspector General, Report, *The Threat and Local Observation Notice (TALON) Report Program* (Washington, DC: Government Printing Office, 2007), i.

[261]Ibid.

[262]Ibid., ii.

reports, the value of the information was not evaluated prior to distribution.[263] Among the TALON reports distributed was notification of a meeting of activists at a Quaker Meeting House who planned to protest high school recruiters.[264] In addition, another TALON Report concerned a planned political protest in Los Angeles, far away from any military installation or recruiting station.[265]

The rapidly expanding program also led to targeting of academic institutions. For example, in a 2004 article, the *Wall Street Journal* reported an incident in which Army lawyers attending a University of Texas Law School legal conference allegedly notified Army intelligence about suspicious comments made by "three Middle Eastern men."[266] After reporting the incident, an Army intelligence agent questioned students and the Dean of Student Affairs, and requested a video copy of the conference.[267] In another case, in 2005, CIFA received and stored e-mail communications in TALON related to "college students who were planning protests against the war in Iraq and against the military's

---

[263]Embedded within a TALON report is the following disclaimer: "This TALON report is not fully evaluated information. . . . This information is being provided only to alert commanders and staff to potential terrorist activity or apprise them of other force protection information." American Civil Liberties Union, News Release, "Document Confirms that RI Peace Protest Was Entered in Federal Terrorism Database," (TALON Report 902-10-12-04-201), 1 November 2006, http://www.riaclu.org/documents/ RICCPTALONdoc.pdf (accessed 22 April 2010).

[264]Myers, et al., "Is the Pentagon Spying on Americans?"

[265]Ibid.

[266]Block and Fields, "Is Military Creeping Into Domestic Spying and Enforcement?"

[267]Ibid.; Schwarz and Huq, 134.

'don't ask, don't tell' policy on gay and lesbian members of the armed forces."[268] The

information related to protests at five separate universities over the course of 2005.[269]

Critics immediately argued that such targeting resulted in a chilling effect on academic

institutions.

The rapid expansion of CIFA's information-gathering initiative came to an abrupt

halt in December 2005. An MSNBC news report on the TALON program revealed the

DoD's role in collecting domestic intelligence.[270] Aside from reporting the incidents

described above, MSNBC reportedly obtained a classified document that suggested DoD

was collecting information on individuals present at the protests, as well as vehicle

descriptions.[271] In response to these explosive allegations, members of Congress asked

the DoD Inspector General (DoD IG) to conduct an internal investigation.[272]

After an eighteen month investigation, the DoD IG found that CIFA's activities

were legal largely because they were collecting raw information, not intelligence.[273] The

---

[268]Henig, A.21; Schwarz and Huq, 134.

[269]The universities included: "Southern Connecticut State University, the State University of New York at Albany, the University of California at Berkeley, and Williams Paterson University of New Jersey." Henig, A.21. In addition, a planned protest against military recruiters at the University of California at Santa Cruz resulted in a congressional inquiry. Department of Defense Inspector General, Report, *The Threat and Local Observation Notice (TALON) Report Program*, ii.

[270]Myers, et al., "Is the Pentagon Spying on Americans?"

[271]Ibid.

[272]Department of Defense Inspector General, Report, *The Threat and Local Observation Notice (TALON) Report Program*, 17-20.

[273]Ibid., i.

report did, however, cite CIFA for failing to follow DoD Directive 5200.27, which requires that information "shall be destroyed within 90 days unless its retention is required by law."[274] The report concluded that CIFA failed to review the unverified information in a timely manner and purge the information that was not relevant to force protection or another DoD purpose. While the investigation was being conducted, DoD took additional steps to respond to public criticism. In March 2006, Deputy Secretary of Defense Gordon England issued guidance that TALON Reports were to be used "only to report information regarding possible international terrorist activity."[275] As a result of this restriction, TALON reports dropped from 49 per month to an average of seven per month.[276] Finally, shortly before the DoD IG report was released, DoD announced that they would shut down the TALON database altogether in light of "its image in Congress and the media."[277] Almost a year later, both CIFA and the JPEN system that supported TALON were also shuttered.[278] In effect, DoD determined that TALON could not be rehabilitated in the eyes of the public and the government, and took preemptive action to eliminate the program.

---

[274]Department of Defense, Directive 5200.27.

[275]Department of Defense Inspector General, Report, *The Threat and Local Observation Notice (TALON) Report*, 32-33.

[276]Ibid., 13.

[277]Ibid.

[278]Burns, "Pentagon Will Close Antiterror Database"; Department of Defense, News Release, "DoD Activates Defense Counterintelligence and Human Intelligence Center."

Post-11 September Lessons

Although the abuses of Vietnam-era Army intelligence were staggering in comparison to the Post-11 September CIFA initiatives, the parallels between the two case studies are notable. In both cases, the rapid expansion of DoD domestic intelligence gathering led to ill-defined boundaries. In addition, like Vietnam-era domestic intelligence, the government relied on the DoD to produce the evidence because of its substantial resources. Finally, the policy determinations made in the wake of 11 September were later changed because of over-aggressive interpretations. The lessons of the Vietnam-era domestic intelligence programs were learned again post-11 September, although DoD was able to remedy the issues before they became as widespread as Vietnam-era experiences. Specifically, Post-11 September domestic intelligence once again revealed three lessons: vague guidance and sweeping authority often leads to abuses; the government continues to look to the military to solve problems because of its significant assets; and the government often comes to regret policy determinations made during times of crisis.

Much like Vietnam-era intelligence issues, the first underlying problem with Post-11 September domestic intelligence was the vague guidance and sweeping authority provided to the DoD. As the Deputy Chief of Staff for Intelligence made clear in the months following the attacks, "Army intelligence may always receive information, if only to determine its intelligence value and whether it can be collected, retained, or disseminated in accordance with governing policy."[279] This statement was reinforced by

---

[279]Noonan, 1

87

GEN Eberhart, NORTHCOM Commander, when he was quoted as saying "It is important to 'not just look out, but we're also going to have to look in,'. . . 'we can't let culture and the way we've always done it stand in the way.'"[280] Following these statements, the DoD received thousands of reports that had little connection to force protection on subjects ranging from political protests to student e-mail transmissions. When the analysts who collected this information failed to dispose of it within DoD intelligence oversight time limits, the revelation that such information was being stored by DoD was an embarrassment to the Department. In retrospect, DoD should have been more discerning in its collection guidance, much like it did in clarification Directives sent after the TALON program was criticized in the press.[281]

In addition to vague guidance, the government's reliance on DoD's substantial intelligence assets also led to the rapid domestic intelligence expansion. As highlighted above, in the months after 11 September 2001, the President established an entire combatant command dedicated to the defense of the Homeland. Within this organization, CIFA, with a budget of over $1 billion over four years, rapidly provided the domestic intelligence needed by both internal and external customers. This almost instantaneous expansion was only possible because the DoD already managed the majority of intelligence assets, so granting them a mechanism to compile and share this information with other agencies was a logical decision. However, the government soon realized that

---

[280]Block and Fields, "Is Military Creeping Into Domestic Spying and Enforcement?" GEN Eberhart later clarified his remarks, stating: "We are not going to be out there spying on people,'. . . 'we get information from people who do.'" Ibid.

[281]Department of Defense Inspector General, Report, *The Threat and Local Observation Notice (TALON) Report Program*, 32-33.

domestic intelligence was vulnerable to "mission creep" once the DoD began collecting it. One Defense Department official stated, "'[The military] started with force protection from terrorists, but when you go down that road, you soon are into everything . . . where terrorists get their money from, who they see, who they deal with.'"[282] The more DoD distributed domestic information to federal and local law enforcement, the more the agencies requested. This phenomenon soon mushroomed into the collection and distribution of information collateral to the DoD's force protection mission. Just as Vietnam-era intelligence expanded because of external requests, Post-11 September domestic intelligence expanded because of requests from federal and local law enforcement.

The final lesson from the Post-11 September expansion of DoD domestic intelligence is that policy crafted during times of crisis is often regretted later. The attacks of 11 September 2001 were unprecedented in our history. The entire Nation united in defense of the homeland, and the government, and specifically DoD, enjoyed widespread support. However, the decision to create a counter-intelligence agency within the DoD that would manage a database consisting of reports collected from military members across the country was ill-considered in retrospect. Although force protection is a legitimate and crucial function of DoD, both CIFA and TALON smacked of the Army intelligence activities of the Vietnam era. Coupled with vague guidance on the parameters of domestic intelligence collection, CIFA was a public relations problem waiting to happen. Although no legal violations occurred, DoD was clearly tone-deaf to

---

[282]Schwarz and Huq, 133-134.

the public's predictable opposition to CIFA activities. Just like the other aspects of this case study, the government forgot the hard-taught lessons of Vietnam-era intelligence when designing Post-11 September DoD domestic intelligence.

Conclusion

The three case studies discussed above reinforce two major points. First, these case studies, played out over the course of the past ninety years, illustrate remarkably similar problems. In each case, the military and civilian authorities struggled with the appropriate balance between leveraging all available intelligence assets to protect the homeland while adhering to the PCA and the spirit of the act. In each case, either the PCA or the principles of the PCA (civilian control of military activities) influenced both the public's perception and the decisions made by government officials related to military domestic intelligence gathering activities. In addition, each of these cases reinforces the need for clearly defined parameters for military involvement in domestic affairs. These parameters serve to both insulate the military from domestic intelligence mission creep while providing clear guidelines to civilian authorities on the limitations of military intelligence. Without these clearly delineated boundaries, civilian authorities may be tempted to assign the military with an ever-expanding role in domestic intelligence, an area that is ripe for mission creep. In addition, as the case studies illustrate, the military is extremely capable, well-resourced, and eager to assist in homeland security missions. As a result, clearly defined limitations like the PCA keep the military from unconsciously foraying into areas better left to civilian law enforcement.

Information-Sharing, the PCA, and Civil-Military Relations

Having established that the PCA does indeed inhibit DoD information-sharing, this subsection argues that such inhibitions are necessary to preserving healthy civil-military relations. In fact, the underlying purpose of the PCA is to preserve the civilian control over military activities. As previously discussed, the government has long struggled with the balance between leveraging all assets available to protect the homeland with the need to preserve our longstanding tradition of civilian control over the military. The recent initiatives related to information-sharing strikes at the heart of this issue. From one perspective, the United States certainly should not be artificially handicapped by the PCA, sentenced to a stove-piped intelligence infrastructure that cannot be fully leveraged to protect the homeland. However, as the case studies have made clear, when the military becomes too involved in domestic intelligence, the military's reputation is often damaged and the specter of a military state soon emerges. This subsection will explore whether the restrictions posed by the PCA are appropriate considering the current threats to the homeland. Central to this analysis will be an explanation of the basic principles of civil-military relations. Then, this subsection will explore how the PCA preserves the sensitive balance between the civilian and military authorities, and how the inter-relationship between the PCA and DoD information-sharing informs on the greater issue of healthy civil-military relations in the United States.

Civil-Military Relations Principles

The PCA can be viewed as a tangible example of the greater principle of civil-military relations. Although there are several interpretations of traditional U.S. civil-military relations, the "normal" theory of civil-military relations holds "that there should be a division of labor between soldiers and statesmen. Political leaders should develop objectives, provide resources, set broad parameters for action, and select a commander-- then step back, and intervene only to replace him should he fail at his task."[283] However, striking a healthy balance is more difficult than it appears at first blush. Although the United States has recently struggled with the correct balance between security in an age of terrorism and preservation of individual liberties, this tension is not new to civil-military relations.

At its foundation, civil-military relations involve the challenge of reconciling "a military strong enough to do anything the civilians ask them to with a military subordinate enough to do only what civilians authorize them to do."[284] For example, although the military is frequently lauded for its domestic disaster recovery capabilities, society is opposed to having those same forces conduct law enforcement duties during these operations. This fine distinction is not without good reason: if the military is the only entity within our civil society that has overwhelming coercive power, this power could potentially be used against the people it was created to protect.[285] Although a traditional military coup seems unlikely in the United States, one of the most disturbing aspects of the military's intelligence activities in the case studies was the collection of

---

[283]Eliot A. Cohen, "Supreme Command in the 21st Century," *JFQ* (Summer 2002): 49.

[284]Peter Feaver, "Civil Military Problematique: Huntington, Janowitz, and the Question of Civilian Control," *Armed Forces & Society* 23, no. 2 (Winter 1996): 149.

[285]Ibid., 152.

information on political groups. The mere prospect that this information could be used to influence the political process could drastically compromise U.S. civil-military relations.

Although civil-military relations enjoyed an intellectual resurgence recently, the two principle theories in this field date back to the 1950s. In his seminal work, *The Soldier and the State*, Samuel Huntington attempted to resolve the inherent tension between building a strong military while preserving civilian authority. As outlined above, he argued a theory of "objective civilian control," in which the civilian authorities dictate military policy, then allow the military decide the military operations necessary to achieve that policy.[286] Central to this theory is an understanding of liberal theory, in which the primary concern of the state is to protect the individual rights of the citizen.[287] As Huntington argues, the major shortfall of liberal theory is that it does not account for the state's duty to secure its citizens from external threats. As a result, the military must be strong enough to defeat external threats, while still being subservient to civilian authority. As such, the only way for objective civilian control to operate effectively in a liberal society like the United States is for the military to be comprised of professional officers who will obey civilian control.[288]

---

[286]Samuel P. Huntington, *The Soldier and the State: The Theory and Politics of Civil-Military Relations* (Cambridge: Belknap Press, 1957); James Burk, "Theories of Democratic Civil-Military Relations," *Armed Forces & Society* 29, no. 1 (Fall 2002): 7.

[287]Huntington, 149. As Huntington explains, the traditional functions of a liberal state are: "the political function of adjusting and synthesizing the interests within society; the legal function of guaranteeing the rights of the individual; and the economic and social function of broadening the opportunities for individual self-development." Ibid.

[288]Burk, 10.

In responding to Huntington's theory, Morris Janowitz advanced the civic republican theory. Janowitz argued that instead of individual rights, the primary focus of a democratic state should be "engaging citizens in the activity of public life."[289] By involving the citizenry in the operation of the state, it expands the interest of the citizen from an interest in common, rather than individual, welfare. In addition, when citizens serve in the military, the interests of the military and civilian society overlap, thereby reducing fear of a military coup.[290] As a result, the civil republican theory was primarily concerned with keeping citizens involved in the military even when a large standing military is not needed.

The PCA as a Microcosm of Civil-Military Relations Problems

Although several scholars have criticized both the liberal and civic republican theories as deeply flawed, they continue to serve as the foundation of civil-military relations.[291] Both theories serve to illustrate the civil-military relations tension inherent in the PCA: the United States places a premium on individual rights and liberties. Out of necessity, citizens surrender limited authority to govern the United States to elected and accountable representatives. This elected government, however, must further delegate responsibility for protecting the citizenry to the military, an entity that is not elected nor

---

[289]Morris Janowitz, *The Professional Soldier: A Social and Political Portrait* (New York: Free Press, 1971); Burk, 10.

[290]Burk, 10.

[291]Ibid.

94

as accountable to the citizens.[292] As a result, the military is restricted in its law enforcement activities, particularly in domestic operations, by laws such as the PCA.

As the case studies made clear, whether an actual or merely perceived PCA violation occurs, irreparable damage can occur. For example, when Army intelligence targets political groups, regardless of motivation, the specter of military interference with the political process usually follows. Whether it is federal troops interfering with the Presidential election in the Reconstruction South or Army intelligence officers observing anti-war protesters, the military must tread cautiously. As the Post-Vietnam case study revealed, Army domestic intelligence upset the civil-military relations balance for many years following the intelligence operations. Not only did it contribute to a widespread anti-military sentiment, but it resulted in a Congressional investigation and complete overhaul of the intelligence structure. What started as a legitimate military mission quickly developed into a scandal with far-reaching effects. Unfortunately, this type of scandal has been replayed on a relatively regular basis throughout the history of domestic military intelligence.[293]

Information sharing is a necessary component of U.S. homeland security. Only by leveraging the considerable intelligence assets available at all levels can the United States hope to safeguard its citizens. Because DoD controls the vast majority of the intelligence resources at the federal level, they will continue to be inextricably linked to domestic intelligence operations. This relationship is wrought with peril as DoD strives to satisfy

---

[292]Feaver, 152.

[293]*The Church Report*, Book 6.

the many needs of its external customers, while simultaneously collecting information related to force protection. Although the DoD may not actually violate the PCA in satisfying these various information requests, the perception of DoD acting in a law enforcement capacity can be just as damaging. If the public perceives the DoD is using information-sharing as a subterfuge to collect and disseminate information it could not otherwise legally obtain, the delicate civil-military relations balance could be upset.

The most important justification for PCA limitations continues to be the preservation of traditional civil-military relations. Although the PCA was originally passed in response to perceptions that federal troops had interfered with state elections in the Reconstruction South, the law has remained relevant because of what it represents. The PCA now reflects the public's firm belief that the military should play a limited role in domestic operations.[294] Despite the numerous exceptions to the PCA that have expanded the military's role in domestic operations, the PCA remains a tangible reminder of the sensitive relationship between the military and society. This relationship is even more sensitive when dealing with domestic intelligence. Society's strong belief in privacy and individual rights makes the prospect of domestic military intelligence an unattractive one for many Americans.

---

[294]Matthew J. Morgan, *The American Military after 9/11: Society, State, and Empire* (New York: Palgrave MacMillan, 2008), 109.

CHAPTER 5

CONCLUSIONS AND RECOMMENDATIONS

Conclusions

The Department of Defense plays a crucial role in U.S. homeland security efforts. From CBRNE response to intelligence capabilities, DoD has the capability to respond to the full spectrum of civil support missions. Over the past several years, other Federal agencies, as well as State and local authorities, have come to increasingly rely on these capabilities. Through the substantial efforts of the Executive to foster an effective information sharing environment, these agencies now enjoy unprecedented cooperation. The DNI now has visibility on all intelligence assets, including those of the DoD, and can readily identify gaps and duplications in the intelligence framework.

Despite the substantial benefits of information sharing, there are several limitations that can lead to confusion. Specifically, the DoD operates under a significant limitation--the PCA. The PCA can be viewed as a manifestation of America's deeply held belief in civilian authority over federal military forces. In turn, the PCA has been the basis for many modern restrictions on DoD, including Intelligence Oversight rules and DoD policies. This thesis has provided a glimpse of the true origin of these modern restrictions in an effort to inform the central question of whether the PCA inhibits DoD information-sharing efforts.

Conclusion 1: DoD Must Continue to Play a Role in Domestic Intelligence

The DoD controls the vast majority of intelligence assets in the United States. With this control comes responsibility to assist other Federal agencies in gathering intelligence necessary for the defense of the homeland. The DoD must continue to play a role in domestic intelligence for three reasons: to support the DoD internal needs for domestic intelligence; to support other agencies in their need for domestic intelligence; and to preserve the already-developed intelligence infrastructure.

First, the DoD requires significant domestic intelligence in support of its missions. To continue force protection and protection of designated federal assets, the DoD needs the capability to gather intelligence related to domestic threats. As discussed in chapter 4, it would be unreasonable to expect the military to put Soldiers in danger within the United States simply to avoid domestic intelligence operations. The Fort Hood shooting demonstrates the immediacy of these dangers and the necessity for relevant and timely intelligence on emerging threats.

Secondly, the DoD provides important domestic intelligence to external customers. Both federal agencies and local authorities rely on the significant assets of the DoD for such information. By participating in central databases like eGuardian, the DoD is able to share volumes of information with other agencies that do not possess the capabilities and resources needed to protect against terrorism threats. In addition, the DoD is able to obtain valuable information from local authorities who are in the best position to identify and evaluate threats.

Third, the current intelligence infrastructure makes DoD a crucial player in domestic intelligence. Without their participation, other agencies would lose access to nearly 90 percent of U.S. intelligence assets. For many years, some agency officials argued that the military can continue their participation without subjecting their activities to PCA restrictions. By allowing National Guard forces operating in Title 32 status to conduct otherwise prohibited intelligence functions, the domestic intelligence restrictions applicable to Title 10 forces could theoretically be subverted. However, such circumvention is no longer possible. In June 2008, a National Guard Bureau directive made the DoD policy for Handing U.S. Persons information applicable to the National Guard.[295]

Another possible option would be transferring intelligence assets to other federal agencies. However, past experiences indicate that transferring capabilities piecemeal to other agencies leads to degradation of the overall system and the transferred component. The DoD's current capabilities were designed to work with each other. For instance, intelligence databases were designed to support the processing of information from specific agencies within the DoD intelligence community. If the database is transferred to another agency, it may prove useless without the agencies that populate the database. The current intelligence system is comprised of interdependent systems and capabilities cannot be effectively separated from the system. Based on the mature intelligence structure and the established need for domestic intelligence products, the DoD must continue to play a role in domestic intelligence.

Conclusion 2: The PCA Inhibits DoD
Information Sharing Efforts

Despite effective information sharing, DoD cooperation with other agencies is not limitless. The DoD must abide a myriad of laws and regulations designed to limit the role

---

[295]Department of the Army and the Air Force, National Guard Bureau, Memorandum, "NGB Policy for Handling of U.S. Persons Information"; Department of the Navy, Marine Corps Order 3800.2B.

of federal military forces in domestic operations. The vast majority of these restrictions can be traced back to the American understanding of proper civil-military relations. The PCA, originally a post-Reconstruction effort to remove Federal troops from the South, has come to symbolize the notion of the military's subordinate role to civil authority. Policy decisions have heavily influenced the popular interpretation of these restrictions. The role of federal forces in War Plans White, Post-Vietnam era, and Post-11 September era domestic intelligence demonstrates the public's firm belief in a limited role for federal military forces. Beyond describing the black-letter law, these case studies reflect the spirit of the PCA and civil-military relations.

As chapter 4 made clear, the PCA spawned a myriad of laws and regulations. For instance, the intelligence oversight procedures implemented in the wake of the Church Report were a result of perceived PCA violations by Army Intelligence. Whether the acts of domestic intelligence were in fact violations of the PCA (some were, and some were not) is not particularly relevant. Rather, it was the spirit of the PCA throughout these historical examples that caused widespread and lasting changes to DoD domestic intelligence gathering.

Three overarching constants can be gleaned from the case studies presented. First, in each of the cases, vague guidance led to ill-defined missions. In all of the studies, the military started off collecting domestic intelligence directly related to their military missions. However, in each of the cases, ill-defined guidance led to mission creep, with the military soon conducting operations greatly attenuated from their original mission. As one DoD official noted, this mission creep may be inherent in intelligence collection, where one piece of information can reveal other potential sources, and the web may lead to yet another source.

The cause of this mission creep may also be related to the second constant: over-reliance on military intelligence assets. Since the 1920s, the military has largely had the most resources and personnel of any other government agency. In War Plans White, the Army was the only organization with the manpower necessary to conduct the widespread intelligence needed under the plan. Similarly, in the 1970s, and again in 2001, the military was the only federal entity with the intelligence infrastructure in place to conduct significant domestic intelligence. As a result, both federal and local authorities began to rely on military capabilities to provide the intelligence necessary to protect the homeland.

Finally, all three case studies make clear that initial policy decisions made during times of national crisis are later changed because of overly aggressive techniques. In the case of War Plans White, many believed that the Socialist Movement in the United States could lead to a revolution. As a result, the Army began to target political groups and record political affiliations, a policy later denounced by the public and the government. Similarly, Post-Vietnam era domestic intelligence was greatly curtailed after the Church Report revealed the Army was conducting surveillance of political and religious groups. Although this collection was initially justified by the widespread civil unrest of the 1960s, after the emergency passed, both Congress and the public identified these policies as counter to the PCA. Finally, in the aftermath of the attacks of 11 September 2001, the military played an expanded role in domestic intelligence, collecting and maintaining information in violation of its own regulations. However, with the benefit of time, the military realized the perils of these practices and returned to a more defined domestic intelligence role. As these cases illustrate, domestic intelligence policies expand and contract with the current situation, and these changes are heavily influenced by the public and government's perception of the limitations of the PCA and related laws.

Conclusion 3: The Restrictions Imposed on DoD Information Sharing
by the PCA are Necessary to Preserve Civil-Military Relations

In addition to demonstrating the limitations PCA imposes on information sharing, this thesis also concludes that such limitations are necessary. As discussed in chapter 4, America's brand of civil-military relations is largely in keeping with the "liberal theory" espoused by Samuel Huntington. The theory holds that American's believe the purpose of our democratic government is to protect the individual liberties of its citizens. American's delegate the day-to-day management of the government to their elected leaders, but reserve the right to replace them through election. In turn, the government delegates the sole coercive power in the country to the military. While elected leaders make the overall military policy, the military is given the authority to execute that policy without interference. In exchange for this limited autonomy, the military agrees to be subordinate to civil authority. However, when the military becomes involved in domestic law enforcement and political activities, the public becomes suspicious that the military, with its coercive power and lack of accountability to the electorate, will attempt to supplant civilian authority. As a result, the PCA and accompanying laws are designed to limit the military's involvement in civil affairs.

The case studies illustrated the effect of military involvement in political and civil affairs. In each of the cases, the Army received especially close scrutiny when they began to gather intelligence on political groups. From the Socialist Movement in the 1920s, to demonstrations on war policy and "Don't ask, Don't Tell" in the 2000s, the American people, and in turn elected leaders, actively opposed such activity. The blurring of the lines between civilian and military missions continues, with terrorists being prosecuted in civilian courts based on military intelligence. However, the spirit of the PCA acts as a necessary buffer to maintain a level of separation between military and civil authority. Such a buffer is crucial to the preservation of healthy civil-military relations and enhances the ability of DoD to participate in fighting terror.

Recommendations

While the PCA continues to play a necessary role in limiting DoD information-sharing, this section explores ways to prevent the effects of such limitations from degrading intelligence capabilities. Namely, the DoD must seek and disseminate a clear understanding of their role in domestic intelligence. In addition, the government must design and employ an effective intelligence database to facilitate responsible information sharing. Finally, the DoD must continue to train on domestic operations and domestic intelligence. These recommendations are modest, and reflect the significant work that has already been done to engage the DoD in domestic operations without violating the PCA.

Recommendation 1: Clarification of DoD's Role in Domestic Intelligence

As identified in the case studies, one of the reasons the DoD has run awry of the PCA in the past is ill-defined guidance. In the midst of a crisis, the domestic intelligence mission is often an ad hoc creation with poorly defined limitations on the collection of information. As a result, in all of the case studies, intelligence agents at the tactical level made blunders that had National Strategic effects. For instance, the Army Intelligence officer that visited the University of Texas Law School in 2004 and demanded information related to an Islamic Legal Conference clearly underestimated the effects his request would have on Army Intelligence. His actions demonstrate a fundamental lack of understanding regarding the sensitivity of domestic intelligence. The fact that the conference took place at an academic institution further aggravated the mistake.

In addition to influencing DoD employees, clear regulations will also prevent mission creep. If DoD's domestic intelligence mission is ill-defined, the department will be vulnerable to an ever-expanding list of requests for domestic intelligence assistance from other agencies. The most effective way to prevent such an expansion is to ensure the decision makers understand the DoD mission and that they can articulate this standard to requesting agencies.

Based on these and other instances, the DoD must reaffirm the limitations inherent in domestic intelligence operations. Rather than publishing this guidance in response to scandals, the guidance must be crafted and taught before agents begin their mission. The guidance must reaffirm DoD's limited role in domestic operations: counterintelligence related to foreign terrorist activity and force protection. Through Directives and Regulations, the DoD must make the boundaries clear. To accomplish this, the DoD must conduct a comprehensive review of all of the Directives and Regulations that have evolved over the course of the last ten years in response to prior violations. Consistency will be the key to providing clear guidance.

Recommendation 2: Building Effective
Information-Sharing Platforms

In addition to establishing clear rules for the collection of domestic intelligence, the DoD must play a central role in the design of an effective intelligence database. The eGuardian system can be effective, but DoD must ensure some minimum requirements are satisfied. First, the system must allow for tagging of information, so that users can readily determine who submitted the information and submitters will be accountable for the accuracy of their submission. Such a tagging system is necessary given the large number of agencies contributing to the database. Furthermore, the database must have a reminder system that requires agencies to update unverified reports. Such a system would require the submitting agency to investigate unverified reports and submit an update or delete the information within 90 days. This will prevent situations like those involving the JPEN database in 2005, in which unverified information was retained for several months. Finally, the system must include virtual walls that prevent DoD users from accessing information unrelated to their military mission. Regardless of who collected the information, if DoD employees can access it, then it may result in an intelligence violation. This aspect will be the most difficult to implement because it will require the database maintainers to be well-versed in the limitations imposed by the PCA, intelligence oversight, and DoD directives. Nonetheless, this feature, along with the accountability and information verification features, will result in an effective database that fosters information sharing.

Recommendation 3: Enhanced Training
in Domestic Operations

The final recommendation is to continue training domestic operations at all levels of the military. As Army FM 3-0, *Operations* makes clear: "The Army's operational concept is *full spectrum operations:* Army forces combine offensive, defensive, and stability or civil support operations simultaneously as part of an interdependent joint force."[296] Although local authorities and National Guard troops are the first to respond to civil support missions in the United States, the manual makes clear that Federal military forces must be prepared to conduct civil support operations when called.[297] While placing civil support on par with offense, defense and stability operations is a great start, DoD must continue to train and equip forces for such missions.

As a part of this training, all forces must be trained in the limitations imposed by the PCA and other laws. Given the rapid development and widespread use of sophisticated intelligence capabilities at the tactical level, military leaders at all levels must understand the limits on domestic intelligence-gathering within U.S. boundaries. In addition, Soldiers must be familiar with the significant difference in intelligence collection and use of force rules in domestic operations versus those in contingency operations.[298] Without this training, Soldiers will default to the training they receive for contingency operations abroad. Soldiers have come to rely on intelligence assets to

---

[296]Department of the Army, Field Manual (FM) 3-0, *Operations* (Washington, DC: Government Printing Office, February 2008), 3-2.

[297]Department of the Army, FM 3-0, *Operations*, 3-99.

[298]For a discussion of the difference between domestic rules for the use of force and operational rules of engagement, see Sennott, 65.

provide situational awareness on the battlefield, but they must be taught that such information may not be as readily available in a domestic setting.

The recommendations listed above are simply refinements to an already sophisticated domestic intelligence framework. As this thesis has demonstrated, the PCA provides necessary limitations on the sharing of information between DoD and its federal and local partners. With clear direction, an effective information-sharing platform, and increased training in domestic operations, the DoD can prevent overstepping the firmly rooted boundaries between civil and military authority.

BIBLIOGRAPHY

Books

Bidwell, Bruce W. *History of the Military Intelligence Division, Department of the Army General Staff: 1775-1941*. Frederick: University Publications of America, 1986.

Blackstone, William. *Commentaries on the Laws of England*. 1765. Book I. Reprint, Birmingham: Legal Classics Library, 1983.

Bloor, Michael and Fiona Wood. *Keywords in Qualitative Methods: A Vocabulary of Research Concepts*. London: SAGE Publications, 2006.

Carey, Neil G., ed. *Fighting the Bolsheviks: The Russian War Memoir of Private First Class Donald E. Carey, U.S. Army, 1918-1919*. Novato: Presidio Press, 1997.

Chamberlain, William Henry. *The Russian Revolution*. New York: The Universal Library, 1965.

Congressional Quarterly. *Presidential Elections: 1789-2004*. Washington, DC: CQ Press, 2005.

Currier, Donald J. *The Posse Comitatus Act: A Harmless Relic from the Post-Reconstruction Era or a Legal Impediment to Transformation?* Carlisle: Strategic Studies Institute, 2003.

Delk, James. *Fires and Furies: The L.A. Riots: What Really Happened*. Palm Springs: ETC Publications, 1995.

Gentry, Curt. *J. Edgar Hoover: The Man and the Secrets*. New York: W.W. Norton & Company, 1991.

Hagedorn, Ann. *Savage Peace: Hope and Fear in America, 1919*. New York: Simon & Schuster, 2007.

Janowitz, Morris. *The Professional Soldier: A Social and Political Portrait*. New York: Free Press, 1971.

Jensen, Joan. *Army Surveillance in America: 1775-1980*. New Haven: Yale University Press, 1991.

Lewis, Jane. "Design Issue." In Ritchie and Lewis, 52.

Matthews, Matt. *The Posse Comitatus Act and the United States Army: A Historical Perspective*. Fort Leavenworth: Combat Studies Institute Press, 2006.

Moley, Raymond, Jr. *The American Legion Story*. Westport: Greenwood Press, 1966.

Moore, Gary W. *Developing and Evaluating Education Research*. Boston: Little, Brown and Company, 1983.

Morgan, Matthew J. *The American Military after 9/11: Society, State, and Empire*. New York: Palgrave MacMillian, 2008.

Myers, Michael D. *Qualitative Research in Business and Management*. Los Angeles: SAGE Publications, 2009.

Pomerantz, Sydney I. "Election of 1876." In Schlesinger, Vol. 2: 1379.

Posner, Richard A. *Uncertain Shield: The U.S. Intelligence System in the Throes of Reform*. Lanham: Rowman & Littlefield, 2006.

Rand Corporation. *The Challenge of Domestic Intelligence in a Free Society*. Edited by Brian A. Jackson. Santa Monica: Rand, 2009.

Ritchie, Jane. "The Applications of Qualitative Methods to Social Research." In Ritchie and Lewis, 34.

Ritchie, Jane and Jane Lewis, ed. *Qualitative Research Practice: A Guide for Social Science Students and Researchers*. London: SAGE Publications, 2003.

Schlesinger, Arthur M. Jr., ed. *History of Presidential Elections*. New York: Chelsea House, 1971.

Schwarz, Frederick A.O. Jr. and Aziz Z. Huq. *Unchecked and Unbalanced: Presidential Power in a Time of Terror*. New York: The New Press, 2007.

Turabian, Kate. *A Manual for Writers*. 7th ed. Chicago: University of Chicago Press, 2007.

Government Documents

Assistant to the Secretary of Defense for Intelligence Oversight. "Frequently Asked Questions." http://atsdio.defense.gov/faq.html (accessed 22 April 2010).

———. "Mission and History: Assistant to the Secretary of Defense (Intelligence Oversight)." http://atsdio.defense.gov/ (accessed 22 April 2010).

———. "Reporting of Intelligence Oversight (IO) Questionable Activities." http://atsdio.defense.gov/documents/quickref.html (accessed 20 January 2010).

Best, Richard A. Jr. CRS Report for Congress, *Intelligence Community Reorganization: Potential Effects on DoD Intelligence Agencies*. Washington, DC: Government Printing Office, 2004.

Bowman, Steve. CRS Report for Congress, *Homeland Security: The Department of Defense's Role*. Washington, DC: Government Printing Office, 2003.

Carter, Jimmy. *Foreign Intelligence Surveillance Act of 1978, Statement on Signing S. 1566 Into Law*, in *Public Papers of the Presidents of the United States: Jimmy Carter*. Vol. 2. Washington, DC: Government Printing Office, 1979.

Chairman of the Joint Chiefs of Staff. Instruction 5901.01B, "Joint Staff Inspector General Responsibilities, Procedures, and Oversight Functions." Washington, DC: Government Printing Office, 11 July 2008.

Department of the Air Force. Instruction 14-104, *Oversight of Intelligence Activities*. Washington, DC: Government Printing Office, 16 April 2007.

Department of the Army and the Air Force, National Guard Bureau. Memorandum, "NGB Policy for Handling of U.S. Persons Information." Washington, DC: Government Printing Office, 18 June 2008.

Department of Defense. "Defense.gov Biographies: Paul N. Stockton." http://www.defense.gov/bios/biographydetail.aspx?biographyid=206 (accessed 22 April 2010).

———. Defense Study and Report to Congress, *The DoD Role in Homeland Security*. Washington, DC: Government Printing Office, July 2003.

———. Directive 3025.1, "Military Support to Civil Authorities (MSCA)." Washington, DC: Government Printing Office, 15 January 1993.

———. Directive 3025.12, "Military Assistance for Civil Disturbances (MACDIS)." Washington, DC: Government Printing Office, 4 February 1994.

———. Directive 5105.67, "Department of Defense Counterintelligence Field Activity (DoD CIFA)." Washington, DC: Government Printing Office, 19 February 2002.

———. Directive 5148.11, "Assistant to the Secretary of Defense for Intelligence Oversight." Washington, DC: Government Printing Office, 21 May 2004.

———. Directive 5200.27, "Acquisition of Information Concerning Persons and Organizations Not Affiliated with the Department of Defense." Washington, DC: Government Printing Office, 7 January 1980.

———. Directive 5240.01, "DoD Intelligence Activities." Washington, DC: Government Printing Office, 27 August 2002.

———. Directive 5525.5, "DoD Cooperation with Civilian Law Enforcement Officials." Washington, DC: Government Printing Office, 15 January 1986 (incorporating change 1, 20 December 1989).

———. "DoD Dictionary of Military Terms." http://www.dtic.mil/doctrine/ dod_dictionary/ (accessed 22 April 2010).

———. News Release, "DoD Activates Defense Counterintelligence and Human Intelligence Center." 4 August 2008. http:www.defense.gov/releases/ release.aspx?releaseid=12106 (accessed 22 April 2010).

———. *Unified Command Plan.* Washington, DC: Government Printing Office, 2008.

———. *Report of the DoD Independent Review, Protecting the Force: Lessons from Fort Hood.* Washington, DC: Government Printing Office, January 2010.

Department of Defense Inspector General. Report, *The Threat and Local Observation Notice (TALON) Report Program.* Washington, DC: Government Printing Office, 2007.

Department of Homeland Security. Office of the Inspector General. *Homeland Security Information Network Could Support Information Sharing More Effectively.* Washington, DC: Government Printing Office, June 2006.

Department of Justice. *Fusion Center Guidelines: Developing and Sharing Information and Intelligence in a New Era.* Washington, DC: Government Printing Office, 2006.

———. "Privacy & Civil Liberties: Federal Statutes Relevant in the Information Sharing Environment." http://www.It.ojp.gov/ default.aspx?area=privacy&page=1283 (accessed 20 January 2010).

Department of the Navy. Instruction 3820.3E, "Oversight of Intelligence Activities within the Navy (DON)." Washington, DC: Government Printing Office, 21 September 2005.

Department of the Navy, Marine Corps. Order 3800.2B, "Oversight of Intelligence Activities." Washington, DC: Government Printing Office, 20 April 2004.

Department of State, Office of the Historian, Bureau of Public Affairs. "History of the National Security Council: 1947-1997." http://ftp.fas.org/irp.offdocs/ NSChistory.htm (accessed 10 January 2010).

Director of National Intelligence. "About the Intelligence Community: A Complex Organization United Under a Single Goal: National Security." http://www.intelligence.gov/about-the-intelligence-community/structure/ (accessed 19 April 2010).

———."News Release: DNI Releases Budget Figure for 2009 National Intelligence Program." 30 October 2009. http://www.dni.gov/ press_releases/20091030_release.pdf (accessed 20 April 2010).

———. United States Intelligence Community: Information Sharing Strategy. Washington, DC: Government Printing Office, 2008.

Doyle, Charles. CRS Report for Congress, *The USA Patriot Act: A Legal Analysis*. Washington, DC: Government Printing Office, 2002.

Elsea, Jennifer K. and R. Chuck Mason. CRS Report for Congress, *The Use of Federal troops for Disaster Assistance: Legal Issues*. Washington, DC: Government Printing Office, 2008.

Executive Order no.11,905. *U.S. Congressional and Administrative News*, vol. 5, 7703 (1977).

Executive Order no.12,333. *Code of Federal Regulations*, title 3, 200 (1982).

Executive Order no.13,228. *Code of Federal Regulations*, title 3, 796 (2002).

Executive Order no.13,284. *Code of Federal Regulations*, title 3, 161 (2004).

Executive Order no.13,311. *Code of Federal Regulations*, title 3, 245 (2004).

Executive Order no.13,355. *Code of Federal Regulations*, title 3, 218 (2005).

Executive Order no.13,356. *Code of Federal Regulations*, title 3, 223 (2005).

Executive Order no.13,388. *Code of Federal Regulations*, title 3, 198 (2006).

Executive Order no. 13,470. *Federal Register* 73, no. 150 (4 August 2008): 45325.

Headquarters, Department of the Army. Command and General Staff College Student Text 20-10, *Master of Military Art and Science (MMAS) Research and Thesis*. Ft. Leavenworth, KS: Command and General Staff College, July 2009.

———. Field Manual (FM) 2-22.2, *Counterintelligence*. Washington, DC: Government Printing Office, 2009.

———. Field Manual 3-0, *Operations*. Washington, DC: Government Printing Office, February 2008.

———. Regulation 381-10, *U.S. Army Intelligence Activities*. Washington, DC: Government Printing Office, 3 May 2007.

Joint Chiefs of Staff. Joint Publication (JP) 3-28, *Civil Support*. Washington, DC: Government Printing Office, 2007.

———. Joint Publication (JP) 3-27, *Homeland Defense*. Washington, DC: Government Printing Office, 2007.

———. Joint Publication (JP) 2-0, *Joint Intelligence*. Washington, DC: Government Printing Office, 2007.

Kaiser, Fredrick M. CRS Report for Congress, *Congressional Oversight of Intelligence: Current structure and Alternatives*. Washington, DC: Government Printing Office, 2008.

Masse, Todd, Siobhan O'Neill, and John Rollins. CRS Report, *Fusion Centers: Issues and Options for Congress*. Washington, DC: Government Printing Office, 2008.

National Counterterrorism Center. "About the National Counterterrorism Center." http://www.nctc.gov/about_us/about_nctc.html (accessed 19 April 2010).

National Geospatial Intelligence Agency. Instruction 8900.4R5, "NGA Instruction for Intelligence Oversight." Washington, DC: Government Printing Office, 30 March 2006.

Noonan, Lieutenant General Robert W. Memorandum, "Collecting Information on U.S. Persons." Washington, DC: Government Printing Office, 5 November 2001.

Senate Select Committee. Final Report of the Select Committee to Study Governmental Operations with respect to Intelligence Activities. 94th Cong., 2d sess., 1976. S. Rep. 94-755.

The United States Commission on National Security/21st Century. *Road Map for National Security: Imperative for Change*. Washington, DC: Government Printing Office, 2001.

United States Government Accountability Office. *Homeland Defense: U.S. Northern Command has a Strong Exercise Program, But Involvement of Interagency Partners and States Can Be Improved*. Washington, DC: Government Printing Office, 2009.

United States Northern Command. "About U.S. NORTHCOM." http://www.northcom.mil/About/index.html (accessed 17 April 2010).

———. News Release, "JPEN Shares Antiterrorism Information Across Nation." 3 March 2004. http://www.northcom.mil/News/2004/030304.html (accessed 22 April 2010).

———. News Release, "U.S. Northern Command Gains Dedicated Response Force." 30 September 2008. http://www.northcom.mil/News/ 2008/093008.html (accessed 19 April 2010).

United States Senate Committee on Governmental Affairs. *Summary of Intelligence Reform and Terrorism Prevention Act of 2004*. Washington, DC: Government Printing Office, 2004.

U.S. National Commission on Terrorist Attacks Upon the United States. *The 9/11 Commission Report: Final Report*. Washington, DC: Government Printing Office, 2004.

The White House. "Fact Sheet: The Protect America Act of 2007." 6 August 2007. http://georgewbush-whitehouse.archives.gov/news/releases/2007/08/20070806-5.html (accessed 21 January 2010).

————. *National Strategy for Information Sharing: Successes and Challenges in Improving Terrorism-Related Information Sharing*. Washington, DC: Government Printing Office, 2007.

————. "President's Radio Address." 17 December 2005. http://georgewbush-whitehouse.archives.gov/news/releases/2005/12/20051217.html (accessed 21 January 2010).

Internet Sources

American Civil Liberties Union. "What's Wrong with Fusion Centers?" http://aclu.org/pdfs/privacy/fusioncenter_20071212.pdf (accessed 27 April 2010).

————. News Release, "Document Confirms that RI Peace Protest was Entered in Federal Terrorism Database." 1 November 2006. http://www.riaclu.org/documents/RICCPTALONdoc.pdf (accessed 22 April 2010).

Bill Moyers Journal. "The Church Committee and FISA." Public Broadcasting System, 26 October 2007. http://www.pbs.org/moyers/journal/10262007/profile2.html (accessed 12 April 2010).

CNN.com. "What is in the New Intelligence Bill." 9 July 2008. http://www.cnn.com/2008/POLITICS/07/09/fisa.explainer/index.html?iref=allsearch (accessed 22 April 2010).

Debree, Jordan and Lee Wang. "Frontline: The Enemy Within: Defending the Home Front: The Military's New Role." Public Broadcasting System. http://www.pbs.org/wgbh/pages/frontline/enemywithin/reality/military/html (accessed 22 April 2010).

Federation of American Scientists. "Intelligence Resource Program: Military Intelligence." http://www.fas.org/irp/offdocs/int014.html (accessed 20 January 2010).

Myers, Lisa, Douglas Pasternak, Rich Gardella, and the NBC Investigative Unit. "Is the Pentagon Spying on Americans?" *MSNBC.com*, 14 December 2005. http:/www.msnbc.comd/10454316/ (accessed 20 April 2010).

PBS Online NewsHour. "An Online NewsHour Report: Air Force General Ralph Eberhart." Public Broadcasting System, 27 September 2002. http://www.pbs.org/ newshour/terrorism/ata/Eberhart.html (accessed 20 April 2010).

Shaughnessy, Larry. "Army Combat Unit to Deploy within U.S." *CNN.com*, 3 October 2008. http://edition.cnn.com/2008/US/10/03/army.unit/index.html (accessed 19 April 2010).

Young, Stephen. "The Posse Comitatus Act: A Resource Guide." 17 February 2003. http://www.llrx.com/features/posse.htm (accessed 20 January 2010).

Journals and Periodicals

Burk, James. "Theories of Democratic Civil Military Relations." *Armed Forces & Society* 29, no. 1 (Fall 2002): 7-29.

Cohen, Eliot A. "Supreme Command in the 21st Century." *JFQ* (Summer 2002): 48-54.

Feaver, Peter. "Civil Military Problematique: Huntington, Janowitz, and the Question of Civilian Control." *Armed Forces & Society* 23, no. 2 (Winter 1996): 149-178.

Henig, Samantha. "Pentagon Surveillance of Student Groups Extended to Scrutinizing E-mail." *The Chronicle of Higher Education* 52, no. 46 (21 July 2006): A.21.

Kealy, Sean J. "Reexamining the Posse Comitatus Act: Toward a Right to Civil Law Enforcement. *Yale Law and Policy Review* 21 (Spring 2003): 383.

Locher, James R III. "The Most Important Thing: Legislative Reform of the National Security System." *Military Review* 88, no. 3 (May-June 2008): 20.

Pyle, Christopher H. "CONUS Intelligence: The Army Watches Civilian Politics." *Washington Monthly* (January 1970): 4-16.

Sennott, Daniel J. "Interpreting Recent Changes to the Standing Rules for the Use of Force." *The Army Lawyer* (November 2007): 65.

Warren, Charles. "New Light on the History of the Federal Judiciary Act of 1789." *Harvard Law Review* 37 (November 1923): 49.

Other Sources

Gentry, Colonel Chris R. "Self-Evident Truths: Why We Can Stop Worrying and Love the Posse Comitatus Act." Research Paper, Army War College, 2008.

Nagl, John A. "Asymmetric Threats to U.S. National Security to the Year 2010."
Master's thesis, Command and General Staff College, 2001.